ABOUT THE AUTHORS

Mildred and Luverne Tengbom bring a rich blend of experience to the writing of this book. Mildred spent seven years as a missionary in India, and she and Luverne together served in Tanzania and Singapore. As parents, their close relationship with God has been a vital part of their family life and continues to bear much fruit. They live in Anaheim, California.

Mildred is a well-known author of many books, including *Table Prayers, Mealtime Prayers, Bible Readings for Mothers,* and *Sing to the Lord*.

Bible Readings
FOR
FAMILIES

Bible Readings

FOR
FAMILIES

Mildred & Luverne Tengbom

AUGSBURG Publishing House • Minneapolis

BIBLE READINGS FOR FAMILIES

Copyright © 1980 Augsburg Publishing House

Library of Congress Catalog Card No. 80-65542

International Standard Book No. 0-8066-1787-X

MANUFACTURED IN THE UNITED STATES OF AMERICA

To

DON AND SANDEE, DAVE AND LINDA
BOB AND CARLA, DAN AND KARYN

who love to be parents
and who have helped us with parenting

PREFACE

Time. How can we find time for all we want to do? Opportunities to learn, grow, develop skills, cultivate friendships, and enjoy the cultural aspects of life abound. Our problem, we say, is to find time for all. Usually our problem is not so much finding time but setting priorities. What is good can easily crowd out what is best.

The enrichment of our spiritual lives through worship, study, prayer, and meditation is often placed near the bottom of our daily "lists" and is therefore neglected. That which is best for us is replaced by things of lesser importance. But we need to turn to God not only for spiritual growth but also for enlightenment and understanding. For life presents us not only with opportunities but also with many complicated and difficult problems.

We are to be grateful that schools and colleges teach courses on problem solving and that trained counselors stand ready to assist us. But the help people can offer through scientific study of human behavior (that which is good) can easily crowd out or even ignore the help God makes available to us (that which is best). That is why concerned Christian parents choose to set aside some time each day for prayer and the reading of God's Word. When this is done also as a family unit, children see their parents praying and turning to God's Word for direction and can participate in this quest.

We have prepared this little book to aid you in directing your families to seek God's help. As we wrote, we often recalled the times we and our four children faced these or similar problems. We hope that after following the short prayer we have included you will go on to voice other concerns of your family. It is our prayer that *Bible Readings for Families* may help you discover some of God's help for you and your family.

Mildred and Luverne Tengbom

■ SHARING OUR TROUBLES

Phil. 4:4-7: "in all your prayers ask God for what you need" (v. 6).

The Simons were having their evening prayer time together, but Lois wasn't ready to pray.

"My teacher just found out her husband has cancer," she said. "She was crying in school today."

"Our baseball team just isn't getting off the ground this year," Tim said. "Some of the guys fight for positions."

"I'm sorry about your teacher," Mom replied, coming back to what Lois had said.

"She's not the only one with troubles," Lois said. "Two of the kids have parents who are getting divorced, and they told us they don't know who they'll be living with."

"Brian says the world's going to come to an end soon," Tim interrupted again.

For the next few minutes Mom and Dad just sat and listened. Then Dad said, "Let's pray about all these things, OK?" He prayed, Tim prayed, Lois prayed, and Mom prayed. When they were all through, Lois sighed happily and said, "I sure feel better!"

Dear God, we can't thank you enough for your love and the opportunity to bring all our concerns to you in prayer.

Before your prayer time, encourage family members to share concerns.

■ WHEN YOU DON'T WIN

Romans 12: "Be happy with those who are happy"
(v. 15).

Lois was in tears. She hadn't been chosen for the softball team.

"They said I can't run fast enough," she sobbed.

Mom sat on the floor beside Lois' bed.

"I'm sorry," she said, "so sorry!"

After a while Lois' sobs subsided.

"Let's pray," Mom suggested. "Dear Lord," she began, "you know what a big disappointment this is for Lois. Help her to do what is really hard to do. Help her to be happy for those who won."

The next day after school Mom heard Lois on the phone.

"Patty? I'm so glad you're going to be a fielder. No, no, don't feel bad I didn't make it. . . . Sure, I wanted to, but not everybody can. . . . No, no, Patty, it's all right. . . . Do you know what I'm going to do? Organize a cheering section! We'll cheer you all on to victory! It'll be a good year, Pat."

Mom smiled. God had performed another miracle. It sure helps to pray!

Dear God, teach us how to accept disappointments and give us grace to be happy for those who win when we lose.

Ask Mom and Dad to share a disappointment they experienced and tell how they handled it.

■ FROM SUPERMARKET TO SINK

Psalm 145:   "Every day I will thank you" (v. 2).

Mom and Dad came into the house carrying brown bags of groceries. Mom thumped her bags down on the table.

"Help me unpack them," she called crossly to Lois, who was watching TV with Tim.

"She's in a bad mood again," Lois whispered to Tim.

"Wonder what the bill totaled this time," Tim whispered back.

At dinner the family bowed their heads as usual and thanked God for their food. But when Tim opened his eyes and saw leftovers, he groaned and said, "I hate leftovers! Why can't we have steak or pizza like Brian's family?"

After dinner Lois tried to sneak away from loading the dishwasher. "I wish we didn't have to eat," she complained when Mom called her back. "Then I wouldn't have to do dishes."

"Time for a family conference again," Dad said.

When they were seated, he asked, "*Are* we really thankful for all the good things God gives us? How about practicing saying table grace or a prayer of thanksgiving all the way from the supermarket to the sink?"

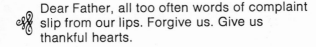
Dear Father, all too often words of complaint slip from our lips. Forgive us. Give us thankful hearts.

Try putting into practice what Dad suggested.

■ THE CAMELS TOO

Gen. 24:15-21:   "I will also bring water for your camels" (v. 19).

Abraham was an old man and very wealthy," Dad said. "But before he died, he wanted to see his son Isaac married to a good girl. It was the custom of that day for parents to choose mates for their children, and they often chose a distant relative to keep family ties strong. So Abraham sent a servant to look for a bride for Isaac. The servant found Rebecca at a well. She was very pretty, but one thing impressed him even more. She offered to draw water for his camels. Look at v. 10. How many camels did he have? Do you know how much water camels can drink? Thirsty camels have been known to drink 30 gallons in 10 minutes. That's a lot of buckets of water to haul up from a well!

"When Isaac's servant heard Rebecca offering to draw water for his camels, he knew she wasn't lazy. She offered to do more than she had been asked to do.

"It's the water we draw for the camels—the extra things that we do—that make our home more than just a place to live," Dad concluded. "When we enjoy doing extra things for others, we all find joy and feel loved."

Dear God, help us discover how much fun it is to do more than we are asked to do.

Discuss ways you can "water each other's camels."

■ BETTER THAN THROWING BRICKS

1 Tim. 2:1-4:   "I urge that petitions, prayers, requests, and thanksgivings be offered to God for all people; for kings and all others who are in authority" (vv. 1-2).

The Simons had guests for dinner, and the adults were talking about politics, inflation, and corruption in the government. This official did this wrong, and that official did that wrong. On and on they went, with their conversation getting more and more dismal.

Finally Lois, who had been sitting quietly but not eating very much, spoke up.

"Daddy," she said. "I remember when our president was elected, he asked us to pray for him. When did we pray for him last?"

Dear God, forgive us for not praying for our leaders but only criticizing them. Give them wisdom. Help them to be honest and to follow in your way.

Find out the names of your state or provincial leaders and the mayor of your city. Write these names down and keep them in a place close to where your family prays together. Send a letter of encouragement and support to some civic leader you feel is doing a good job.

■ DON'T BE A FOOLISH CHICKEN

Prov. 1:20-33: ''Foolish people! How long do you want to be foolish?'' (v. 22).

The gas shortage had changed the Simon's vacation plans.

"We'll go to the campground by the lake," Mom said, "and camp there for a week. I've always wanted to set up camp in one spot and stay there for several days instead of moving every day."

"Brian's dad says the shortages aren't real," Tim said. "He says people just say there isn't any gas so they can make money."

"That reminds me of a story," Dad said. "A mother hen worried about her baby chicks because a chicken hawk kept circling overhead. 'Little chicks,' she said, 'when you hear me cluck, come running and get under my wings.'

"One day the mother hen saw the shadow of the dreaded chicken hawk fall on the ground. 'Cluck, cluck, cluck!' she called. The little chicks came running and hid under her wings. All but one, that is. That little chick said to himself, 'I'll just put my head under my wing, and then I won't see the hawk.' The last that was heard of that little chick as the hawk swooped him away was, 'Help! Help! Help!'

"God wants us to face our problems, not run away from them or pretend they aren't there. He will help us."

Dear God, help us to be wise and not foolish. Give us the courage to face our problems realistically and trust in you.

Discuss ways of spending vacations without using a lot of gasoline.

■ GROWING UP

1 Samuel 1: "She took Samuel, young as he was, to the house of the Lord at Shiloh" (v. 24).

Lois and Tim's five-year-old cousin Nancy was visiting them. One day she didn't want to eat breakfast. She didn't want to eat lunch either.

"Are you sick?" Mom asked.

"No," Nancy answered.

But by midafternoon hunger had won out, and Nancy came in and asked for a sandwich.

"Know why I didn't want to eat?" she asked, hungrily munching her tuna sandwich. "Yesterday when I climbed up in your lap you said I was getting so big that soon you won't be able to hold me." She nibbled an olive and continued shyly, "And I don't want to get so big I can't sit on your lap anymore!"

Mom didn't laugh, but she did smile.

"That's the way growing up is," she said. "We want to, and yet we don't want to. We gain some things and we lose others. But Jesus will help us through it all. When Samuel was left with Eli at the house of the Lord I'm sure he wished he could have stayed home. But God helped Samuel, and he will help you too as you grow up."

 Help us through our growing up years, Lord.

Discuss ways in which you have grown up during the past year.

17

■ LOVE, LOVE, LOVE

1 Corinthians 13: "Love is patient and kind . . . "
(v. 4).

Let's talk about love," Dad said. "Let's take turns and complete the sentence, 'Love is _____.' "

After all the Simons had told what they thought love was, Dad read 1 Cor. 13:4-7. Then he said, "Now let's take turns again and complete another sentence: 'I show my love for God by _____.'
When you complete this sentence," he explained, "describe something you do to show your love for God."

Which sentence do you think was easier for the Simons to complete?

Thank you, God, that you showed your love for us by sending your Son to die for us.

Take turns completing the two sentences above.

■ YOU'RE SO FUSSY!

Matt. 11:28-30: "the yoke I will give you is easy" (v. 30).

Mom, you're so fussy!" Tim complained. "Why do I have to keep my room so clean? And why do I have to make my bed? I'll be crawling into it again tonight, won't I?"

"Tim," said Mom, "what kind of work did Jesus do when he was growing up?"

"I guess he was a carpenter," Tim said.

"Right," said Mom, "and he probably made many things, including yokes for oxen. Do you know what a yoke is?"

"Sort of a collar, isn't it?"

"Yes," said Mom, "so when two oxen pull a load together, one doesn't have to pull harder than the other. Jesus said *his* yoke is easy to wear. That must have been especially meaningful to him, because the yokes he made as a carpenter would have been shaped to fit the neck of each ox."

"Custom built, you mean," offered Tim. He thought for a moment. "Are you trying to tell me that if Jesus did his work so carefully, I should too?"

Mom grinned. "Pride of workmanship," she said.

Dear Jesus, help us to take care of our rooms as though we were expecting Jesus to be our guest tonight.

Think of something your family can do together next Saturday to make your home a nicer place for others.

■ LITTLE LIES

Eph. 4:25-32: "No more lying, then!" (v. 25).

Tim had failed his math exam again.

"Tim, give this letter to your parents, will you, please?" his teacher said as school was dismissed.

Tim's face flushed. "She's tattling on me," he thought.

On the way home he passed an empty trash can. Impulsively he reached in his pocket and then threw the teacher's note in the can.

The next night after dinner Tim's dad asked casually, "Did your teacher give you a note for us yesterday, son?"

"Huh? Naw!" said Tim.

Then Tim's dad put a familiar-looking envelope on the table. "Tim, Mom and I invited your teacher for dinner Friday night, and this was her note saying she could come. One of the neighbors found it in her trash can."

Tim felt his neck get red. After several uncomfortable minutes he explained what had happened. "I guess it's kinda dumb trying to hide things and lie, isn't it?" he asked. "You only hurt yourself."

(each prays silently) Lord, forgive me when I lied to _____. Help me to be truthful.

Discuss what difference it would have made if Tim had not lied.

■ DOES GOD ALWAYS ANSWER PRAYER?

Matt. 7:7-11: "Ask, and you will receive" (v. 7).

Lois sat at the kitchen table sorting index cards.

"What are you doing, Lois?" Mom asked.

"Going through my prayer cards," Lois answered. "This stack," she patted the cards, "are prayers God answered. This stack," she sighed, "he said no to."

"And the cards in your hand?" Mom asked.

"So far God hasn't said either yes or no to these, so I guess I'll keep on praying. Mom, does God always answer prayer?"

"That's a hard question," Mom said. "God always hears us. But he doesn't always give us the things we ask for. Remember how we prayed that your little brother David would live?"

Lois nodded.

"He didn't. But God has given us the courage to go on living without David, and he has blessed us in many other ways. He answered our prayers, but in a different way than we hoped for at the time."

Lois squinted. "It's a mystery, isn't it?" Looking at the cards in her hand, she said, "Anyway, until God tells me otherwise, I'll just keep on praying for these."

Dear God, help us to trust you when we don't get the things we ask for in prayer. Help us to keep on praying when your answers to our prayers seem to be delayed.

Do as Lois did. Write your prayer requests on cards or in a book. Note when God answers them and how he answers them.

■ ME FIRST!

Phil. 2:1-11: "Look out for one another's interests" (v. 4).

Tim and his friends, sweaty and hot from playing baseball, went chasing into Tim's house to make some lemonade.

Tim clink-clunked ice cubes into the glasses and began to pour.

"Me first," yelled Brian, poking his hand under Jimmy's nose.

"Waddya mean? I'm first in line," yelled Jimmy, giving Brian's arm a push.

Crash! Brian's arm had hit Tim's arm and knocked the pitcher to the floor. Lemonade splashed all over the boys' shoes.

"Now see what you did!" Tim cried. "That's what you get for being so selfish! And that was the last can in the frig too."

Selfishness always causes trouble. Selflessness brings happiness. Our Lord Jesus gave his life for others. He is ready to give us his love today so we can overcome our selfishness in order to love and serve others.

Forgive us, Lord, when we are selfish. Thank you that you always give us so much.

Think of one unselfish thing you can do for someone in your family to show them you love them, and then do it.

■ THE TONGUE

James 3:1-12:   "No one has ever been able to tame the tongue" (v. 8).

Have you ever stopped to think what a powerful thing our tongue is? Our tongues can do so many things. Take a minute and talk about some of them.

Think of how we use our tongues to create an atmosphere in our home. If we use our tongues to bicker, tease, sass, scold, criticize, or complain, what kind of atmosphere settles over our home? How do we feel?

But how do we feel if we use our tongues to sing or to say, "Thank you," "I love you," "Please," "I'm sorry," "That's too bad," "I think you're doing great," or "Let's hope tomorrow will be better"? And best of all, if we use our tongues to pray, we open the door for Jesus to help us. Let's do that right now.

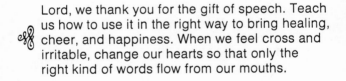

Lord, we thank you for the gift of speech. Teach us how to use it in the right way to bring healing, cheer, and happiness. When we feel cross and irritable, change our hearts so that only the right kind of words flow from our mouths.

Be ready tomorrow night to share something you said during the day that brought happiness to someone.

■ THANK YOU NOTES

Luke 17:11-19 "Why is this foreigner the only one who came back to give thanks to God?" (v. 18).

It was February and Tim's birthday. Tim's grandfather always sent Tim a gift in the mail, but this year no gift had come.

"He forgot," Lois said.

"Grandpa never forgets," Tim said.

"Postage is too high," Dad guessed.

"Tim," Mom asked, "did you send Grandpa a thank-you letter for his Christmas gift to you?"

Silence. Tim squirmed.

"It was only five dollars," he said.

"Only five dollars!" Mom's voice sounded ominous. "Do you know how much that is for your grandpa, living on a fixed income?"

Tim hung his head and crept off to his room. Minutes later he returned.

"Here," he said, giving an envelope to Mom. "Do you have a stamp?"

The doorbell rang.

"This was delivered to our house by mistake," the neighbor girl said, handing Tim a package.

"Grandpa remembered me anyway!" Tim exclaimed. And then he added, "I'll be sure to send him thanks for this one right away!"

 Gracious Lord, teach us to be more thankful.

Write letters of thanks to people who have helped you.

■ WHEN YOU'RE SIZZLIN' MAD

Psalm 4: "In your anger do not sin" (v. 4 NIV).

They make me so mad!" Tim exploded as he came tearing in the house.

"What's up now?" Dad lowered the newspaper and peered at Tim. "Your head's wet," Dad noticed.

Tim was glum.

"Kids douse you with water again?" Lois asked. "They say, 'Shall we put out the fire, Red?'" she explained to her father.

"Makes me so mad!" Tim sputtered. "I . . . I could cuss."

"Martin Luther said sometimes the devil knocked at his door, trying to get him to do something he shouldn't when he was angry," Tim's dad said.

"Oh, yeah?"

"And Luther said he answered the devil by saying, 'Sorry, Martin Luther doesn't live here anymore. Jesus Christ lives here now. Just wait a minute. I'll have him talk to you.'"

Tim grinned. "And then?"

"Then the devil took off."

"That's neat," Tim said. "Think I'll try that too."

Dear God, help us understand how to control our anger so we won't sin when we are angry.

Let each family member complete this sentence: "When I get angry at (or because of) _____, I am tempted to _____. A better way to handle my anger would be _____.

25

■ WHY DO WE GET SICK?

John 11:1-15: "Lord, your dear friend is sick" (v. 3).

Lois was sick. She had chicken pox and mumps at the same time. She itched all over, and she couldn't eat. She was miserable.

"Mom, why do we get sick?" she whimpered when she came in to check her temperature.

"God never meant for us to be sick," her mom said. "He wants us to be well."

"If we pray, won't God make us well?"

"You'll be over your mumps and chicken pox in a few days," Mom said. "But, yes, we can always pray when we get sick. We can ask God to heal us according to his will. Also when we're sick we can ask God to give us patience so we can be cheerful even when we don't feel good."

"I sure need God to help me," Lois confessed, " 'cuz I don't feel good at all."

"I know," Mom soothed, reaching over to kiss Lois. "Jesus understands that too."

Dear Jesus, we pray for _____
who is sick. Heal _____ according
to your will. Give _____ patience.

Send a get-well or cheer-up card to someone you know who is ill or a shut-in. Have all the family members write a sentence on it.

■ WASTING TIME

John 9:1-7: "As long as it is day, we must do the work of him who sent me" (v. 4).

Tim was jealous of his sister Lois. Their dad had said they could go to summer camp if they each contributed $10 to the cost. Lois had earned $10. Tim hadn't.

"You could have," Lois said, "if you hadn't been so lazy. You could have cut lawns or vacuumed for Mom."

"Phooey!" said Tim. He didn't want to talk about it.

Time is a gift from God. We can spend it in many ways. Spending time to earn money for something we want is just one way we can use time.

It is sad if we don't use our time but just sleep it away or let hour after hour pass sitting in front of a TV. Once a day is gone we can never have that time to use again.

When he was on earth, Jesus knew he had only a few years to spend here as a light to people. He said he had his Father's business to do. He will make us wise in spending our time if we ask him to teach us.

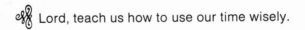 Lord, teach us how to use our time wisely.

Agree that for at least one week each of you will spend a little time in prayer. Check with each other to see how faithful you are, and talk about what difference this prayer time makes for you.

■ FISTS OR DISCUSSION?

Acts 15:1-21: "Paul and Barnabas got into a fierce argument with them" (v. 2).

Tim's softball team was having a big disagreement. Voices got louder and louder. Tim started to dance around the boys, feigning punches. The boys started to punch back. Tim's anger blazed suddenly, and he plowed into the boys, letting his fists fly.

And then a hand grabbed Tim's jacket and lifted him out of the crowd. Tim looked up into the brown eyes of a police officer.

"What's up, young man?"

"Just a little disagreement," Tim said, explaining the problem.

"Well, now, why don't you fellows talk it over with your parents?" the officer said. "That would be a better way to settle an argument, wouldn't it?"

God wants us to live at peace and settle our disputes by talking and coming to some agreement. This is what Paul and Barnabas did when they couldn't agree with some of the other Christians. They went to Jerusalem and talked things over with the Christian leaders there. Together they reached an agreement.

Teach us, Lord, how to settle disputes peacefully.

Think of some issue that has been dividing your family. Talk about it together and try to come to an agreement.

■ SASSING

2 Kings 2:23-25:   "Get out of here, baldy!" (v. 23).

What a dreadful story of the bears that tore up the boys who sassed! But the story still has something to say to us.

Tim's grandmother was driving one day when she had to screech her brakes to avoid hitting some boys who drove their bikes right in front of her. One of them shook his fist at her and yelled, "Stay home where you belong, Grandma!"

Tim's grandmother was angry, but she felt sad also. One day those boys too would be old, she thought. How will they like it when someone yells at them? And why should she stay home? Does the world belong only to the young and healthy?

When Martin Luther taught his children what the commandment "Honor your father and your mother" meant, he explained, "We are to fear and love God so that we do not despise or anger our parents and others in authority, but respect, obey, love, and serve them."

To know we should honor and respect our parents and elders is one thing. To do it is another. God will help all of us, parents and children, if we will trust him. He will help parents to so live and act as to win respect, and he will help children to obey.

Teach us, heavenly Father, to love and to be respectful and courteous toward older people.

Find or draw a picture of children helping older people.

■ THE GRUMPY-GRUMPS

Exod. 16:1-8: "they all complained to Moses and Aaron" (v. 2).

The Israelites were grumbling. When they lived in Egypt they had not been free, but at least they had plenty to eat! God was bringing them to a land of their own where they would be free. But on the way they were forced to give up some things. They complained. They were more interested in being fed than in being God's people.

Lois was grumpy. Her mother wouldn't let her go to a movie her friends were going to because it had too much sex and violence in it. Lois was also grumpy because her allowance wasn't as big as the allowances her friends had. And why did she have to go to church *every* Sunday? It was a bad, grumpy-grump day for Lois, and she was feeling sorry for herself. Today lots of things seemed more important to her than God. She needed to pray.

Dear Jesus, help us to understand that sometimes it costs us to be Christians. Keep us from grumbling.

Find pictures of happy children and grumpy children. Talk about what you think made them happy or grumpy.

■ TATTLING

Exod. 20:16:   "Do not accuse anyone falsely."

Why do kids tattle on each other?
Is it because they are jealous of each other or angry
with someone and want to get even? Or is it because
they think exposing someone else's naughtiness will
make them appear better than the others?

Here are some good questions to ask ourselves
before we tell stories about others:

Am I sure what I am saying is true?

Am I telling this because I really love the person
and want to help him or her?

What difference would it make if I didn't tell?

What difference would it make if I told?

In all our relationships God wants us to love others
and desire their good. This is possible for us when
God puts his love in our hearts. Then we can love
because God is loving others through us.

Dear God, help us to understand when we should
tell things and when we should remain silent.

**Think of some examples when someone has tattled.
Ask the questions above. What conclusions did
you come to?**

A PIG OR A CAT

1 John 1:5-10: "if we confess our sins to God . . . he will forgive us" (v. 9).

Tim limped into the house dragging his jacket. He held it up for his mother to see the ripped-out sleeve.

"Sorry!" he muttered.

She looked at the jacket and then at his muddy face. "Fighting again?"

Tim's head drooped. "I hate myself!" he said. "I get so mad I can't think."

"Tim," Mom said, "You've been to Grandpa's farm. You've seen how the pigs wallow around in the mud, haven't you?"

"I'm no pig!" Tim exploded, pushing back his hair with a muddy hand.

"No, no, I think you're a cat."

"A *cat?*"

"Yes. A cat. Throw our cat into some mud and what would she do? Get out as fast as she can. And then lick herself clean. She doesn't feel at home in mud."

Dear God, some sinful habits are like traps. We get caught in them over and over. Thank you that you never give up on us.

Write down something you need help in overcoming.

■ WHY DO I HAVE TO GO TO CHURCH?

Heb. 10:19-25: "let us come near to God with a sincere heart and a sure faith" (v. 22).

Why do I always have to go to church?" Lois complained. It was early Sunday morning, and sleeping longer sounded a lot more appealing.

"You know," Mom said.

"To learn God's Word, to pray with other Christians, to worship God," Lois said in a singsong voice. Her tone changed. "But God is everywhere. I can worship him wherever I am."

"It's like this," Mom said. "In the summer we like to go to a lake or the beach or the mountains to relax. It's easier to relax in a special place away from our work. We go to a library to study. We go to the doctor's office to see the doctor. And we go to church because it's a special place, set aside just for worshiping him. God *is* everywhere. But in church it's easier for *us* to think about him."

Dear God, forgive us for not wanting to spend more time with you by reading your Word, singing your praises, and praying.

Can your family think of one person you can invite to go with you to church next Sunday?

■ BE THANKFUL

1 Thess. 5:12-24: "be thankful in all circumstances" (v. 18).

Tim and his family were on their way home from the airport. They had just said good-bye to Tim's grandparents.

"Ever notice how Grandma always says, 'Well, it surely isn't worth complaining about?'" Tim asked.

"I know," Mom agreed. "The other day I was sure her arthritis was hurting her. I asked her if her knees were sore. She said, 'If you didn't ask me so many questions, I wouldn't have to tell so many lies!'"

Everybody laughed.

"But Grandma's cheerful spirit and determination to make the best of everything helps her enjoy life as much as she does," Dad observed.

"Humph!" snorted Tim. "It not only helps her; it helps us. Think what we would feel like if she griped all the time about how much she hurt!"

"That's right," Dad said. "And God is always ready to help us give thanks, rejoice, and be cheerful, even when we don't feel like it."

Teach us, Lord, to look on the bright side of things and praise you instead of complaining.

**Can you think of someone who complains a lot?
Is there something nice you could do for that person?**

34

■ DOING MORE THAN YOU'RE ASKED

Matt. 5:38-42: "if one of the occupation troops forces you to carry his pack one mile, carry it two miles" (v. 41).

One day when Tim was taking some of his clothes out of the dryer to fold them, he noticed his mom had thrown in a couple of his dad's shirts. He just dumped those on the floor in a heap.

"Oh, Tim," Mom said later, when she picked up the crumpled shirts, "now I'll have to press these."

Tim just left the room.

But that night he couldn't go to sleep. He kept thinking of the crumpled shirts and how often his mother had laundered, pressed, and hung up his clothes.

The next time his mom tossed a couple of his dad's shirts in with his wash, Tim hung them up. And he felt better too.

We are happiest and feel best about ourselves when we do extra things for people instead of trying to get by with as little as we can.

Dear Jesus, help us see opportunities to do extra things for people.

Write the names of family members on slips of paper. Draw names. Try to do special things for the person you draw without that person finding out who is doing them. At the end of the week have everyone guess who their "secret pals" are.

■ CAN GUNS KEEP US SAFE?

Psalm 91: "He will keep you safe" (v. 3).

Tim stared at the newspaper lying on the kitchen table.

"Dad," he said, putting his finger on an article, "these people who were robbed last night live on the next block!"

Lois crowded next to Tim. "Julie's in my class at school!" she exclaimed. "It was Julie's house!"

"Two men armed with guns . . ." Tim read, "Dad," he said suddenly, "shouldn't we get some guns? You could have one under your pillow, and I could have one. Wouldn't guns keep us safe?"

"Tim," Dad said quietly, "I don't think I want a gun for a pillow. We'll do what we can to make our house safer with locks. But the best thing we can do is tell people about Jesus and show them that we love them. Many people are criminals because no one cares about them or really helps them."

"But how can we help them if we don't even know who they are?" Tim asked.

"Most crimes are committed by the same people, and they are in jail much of the time," Dad answered. "We should find out what our church is doing to visit prisoners and support prison chaplains."

Lord, we thank you that you are a strong and mighty God. We pray that you would watch over us and care for us in times of danger.

Visit with a prison chaplain. Find out what your church is doing in the area of prison ministry.

■ WHY DOESN'T GOD PROTECT US?

James 1:1-18: "consider yourselves fortunate
when all kinds of trials come your way" (v. 2).

I can't understand it," Lois said the next night at
the dinner table. "I was talking with Julie today.
Julie's parents are Christians, and she said they've
asked God to take care of them, but they were
still robbed."

"Sometimes those things happen," Dad said. "Just
because we're Christians doesn't mean bad things
can't happen to us."

"Then what's the use of praying?" Lois asked.

Dad shook his head. "These are hard questions," he
admitted. "They're hard because we don't see things
the way God sees them. We would like God to protect
us from everything that might hurt us, but he sees
value in the trials we face. Lois, if you were going to
compete in a long-distance race, would you just
relax or would you train yourself by running?"

"I'd have to train, or I wouldn't have a chance,"
Lois said.

"That's right," Dad said. "And even though running
often seems painful, it will do you good in the end.
God knows that our faith needs practice. And if
everything were easy for us, we wouldn't grow any
stronger. So even though some things that happen to
us are very painful, they are also opportunities for us
to increase our endurance."

Dear God, help us to trust you even when things
happen to us which we can't understand.

**Pray for someone you know who is going through
a difficult time.**

■ MERCY!

Luke 10:25-37:   "Love your neighbor as you love yourself" (v. 27).

Mercy!" Lois said. She had heard the woman next door say "Mercy!" Then Lois asked, "What does *mercy* mean?"

"Jesus once told a story about mercy," Mom said. "A man was on a journey, traveling on a lonely road. Robbers stopped him, beat him up, and left him for dead. A priest came along and moved way over to the other side of the road to pass him. The next person did the same. But the third person—who was a very ordinary person and a member of a minority group—stopped. He washed the man's wounds and bandaged them. Then he took the man to the nearest inn or hotel. When he left, he said to the clerk at the hotel, 'Send the bill to me.' The third man had mercy on the wounded man."

"Jesus has had mercy on us too," Mom continued. "We are sinners. We do not deserve anything good. But Jesus came and died for us so we might be forgiven and have eternal life."

"Mercy!" Lois said.

Mom smiled. "Yes," she said, "that really was mercy."

We sin every day, dear Jesus. Thank you that you never get tired of having mercy on us.

What works of mercy does your church do?

■ YOU HAVE BEEN REDEEMED

2 Peter 2:1-3: "the Master who redeemed them" (v. 1).

After she got her new 10-speed bike Lois didn't want her old bike anymore, so she gave it to a thrift store. Two days later Lois' new 10-speed bike was stolen from the school parking lot.

"Why did I give my old bike away?" Lois moaned.

She hurried down to the thrift store. Her bike was still there. She bought it back for ten dollars.

That night at dinner Dad said, "We could say that you 'redeemed' your bike, Lois, for that is what the word *redeem* means when we read it in the Bible. God created us. But we sinned and became separated from him. So God bought us back for himself. When Jesus suffered and died for us, he redeemed us."

"Jesus had to pay much more to redeem us than I had to pay to redeem my bike, didn't he?" Lois said soberly.

"Yes," Dad said, "that's why we love him so much."

How can we ever thank you enough for all you've done for us, Jesus? Help us to thank you by helping others.

Are you remembering to put money aside for your Christmas gifts to missions work? When Jesus died, he redeemed not only us but the whole world.

■ HOW TO FORGIVE

Matt. 6:5-15: "If you forgive others . . . your Father in heaven will also forgive you" (v. 14).

I hate Mickey," Lois said. "He says I don't use the right kind of soap, so I stink. He always pushes me when we walk out of the classroom."

"Mickey isn't behaving very nicely," Mom said, "but it won't help you, Lois, if you feel resentful toward him. God wants you to forgive him even if he is mean."

"I hate him," Lois repeated. "I've been thinking about what I could do to get even. If I knew for sure which bike is his, I'd let the air out of his tires."

Mom shook her head. "That won't help a thing. He'll find out and be meaner than ever to you."

At devotions that night they closed with the Lord's Prayer. Then Mom said, " 'Forgive us our sins. . . .' Lois, how do you want God to forgive you?"

Lois just pouted and left the room. But at bedtime she came running to Mom and said, "I just forgave Mickey, and I sure feel better."

Dear God, you have forgiven so many of our sins. Help us to forgive quickly those who do wrong to us.

Think quietly. Is there anyone you feel resentful or angry toward whom you should forgive?

■ REMOVE ONE OR TWO DOMINOES

Romans 12:   "Do everything possible on your part to live in peace with everybody" (v. 18).

I don't hate Mickey anymore," Lois said, "and I'm not going to let air out of his bike tires. But he still says nasty things, and he still pushes me."

"Be patient," Mom said. "Try not to say anything when he teases. When he pushes you, you can say, 'Stop pushing!' and let everyone see what he's doing. The Bible says we should do what we can to get along peaceably with others. But some people just don't want to be agreeable. If you do all you can, you can leave the rest with God. He is the God of peace and love, and he will be with you."

Live in our hearts, Lord Jesus, and give us your Spirit, so we will want to live peaceably with others.

Stand some dominoes up on the table. Push one and watch them all fall. Remove one or two in the middle and then see what happens. Remind yourselves that in the midst of a quarrel, if one person stops talking and arguing, the quarrel soon ends.

■ HONEST AND FAITHFUL WORK

Prov. 3:1-10:   "Never let go of loyalty and faithfulness" (v. 3).

Tim was ready to begin his very first job, delivering
papers. At the dinner table Dad said, "Thomas
Jefferson once said there were three characteristics
employers look for in their employees. The first is,
'Is he honest?' The second is, 'Will he work?' And the
third is, 'Is he loyal and faithful?' You will be a good
employee, Tim, if you remember those three things.
And if you practice honesty, diligence, and faithfulness
now on this job you will benefit from it in the jobs
you have later."

   If we do our work because we love God and as a
way of saying thank you to him for all his goodness to
us, these three things will be evident in our work.
We will be honest, industrious, and faithful. And the
place to begin to work in this way is at home as we
care for our family responsibilities.

Dear God, whatever our work is, help us to do
it as though we were working for you.

**Have a moment of quiet reflection as each family
member asks how he or she can practice honesty,
industriousness, and loyalty.**

■ FLEXIBILITY

Rom. 15:1-6: "We should not please ourselves.
. . . For Christ did not please himself" (vv. 1, 3).

It was family conference time again. With Tim's new job delivering papers in the evening some changes would have to be made. Tim's after-school chores varied from day to day, but they always included sweeping the walks in summer or shoveling them in winter, setting the table for dinner, and feeding the dog.

"You can get up a little earlier in the morning and take care of the walks," Dad said, "and feed the dog when you get home."

Tim frowned. He hated getting up in the morning. That was why he had asked for an afternoon delivery.

"I can't set the table," Lois said hastily. "I have piano practice."

"You can practice earlier," Mom said, "and the day you take your lesson and on Saturdays I'll set the table."

Learning to adapt is one of the most important lessons for a family to learn. Schedules change, and everybody has to change with them. Being willing to help each other and cheerfully adapt will make our homes happier places to live. Jesus helps us by giving us the willingness to change and help each other.

Dear God, we thank you that you have made us capable of changing. Give us the willingness to change when it is needed.

Plant a sweet potato bud or some seeds and watch them grow. As they grow, talk about how change and growth are related.

■ RICHES THAT SATISFY

Matt. 6:19-21: "your heart will always be where your riches are" (v. 21).

Tim crept into Lois' room.

"What were Mom and Dad talking about so loud?" he whispered.

"Money," Lois said. "The charge-card bill came. Six hundred and forty-two dollars."

Tim whistled softly.

"Wow! What all did that include?"

"Some clothes. Some restaurant bills. And a new table for the living room."

"You and Mom spend a lot on clothes."

"And your new 10-speed bike was on it, too" said Lois. "Don't forget *that*."

God knows that owning lots of things can never satisfy us. But if we put Jesus first in our lives, he has promised to take care of all our needs and give us the gifts of contentment and happiness.

Lord Jesus, help us to be satisfied with the salaries our family earns and teach us to spend our money wisely, always remembering to help those who have less than we do.

Talk about things your family could do without so you would have more money to give to those who really need it.

■ WHY DO PEOPLE GET DIVORCED?

Matt. 19:3-9:   "Moses gave you permission to divorce your wives because you are so hard to teach. But it was not like that at the time of creation" (v. 8).

Tim came home from school and banged his books on the table.

"Brian's all shook up," he said. "His mom and dad are getting a divorce. Mom, why do people get divorced?"

Mom was peeling potatoes for dinner.

"You kids always ask such hard questions," she said. "Tim, there are as many reasons for divorce as there are people. I think Brian's parents are divorcing because Brian's father wants to marry someone else."

"Is that OK?"

"No, not according to God's Word. Marriage should be for keeps."

Lois had come in and was listening.

"People get divorced because they can't get along with each other," she said matter-of-factly.

"Sometimes that's true," Mom said. "And there's usually fault on both sides. An unwillingness to say, 'I'm sorry,' or 'Forgive me.' Not talking or listening to each other. Not caring."

Dear God, help _____ who are hurting because of divorce. Help them to make a new life for themselves.

Do you know of someone who has just gone through a divorce whom you can invite over for an evening or for dinner?

■ LEARNING TO ADJUST

Col. 3:12-17: "clothe yourselves with compassion, kindness, humility, gentleness, and patience" (v. 12).

Tim couldn't believe his ears. A baby was crying in their house! Who was visiting them?

"Mary Stuart at church became ill suddenly and had to go to the hospital," Mom said. "I told her I'd take care of her baby."

Tim stared.

Everything seemed to go wrong that night. Mom didn't have time to make supper. The family could eat cold cereal, she said. There was no milk. Mom had forgotten to go to the store. The baby's crib was in Tim's room. Tim didn't want to sleep with the baby. Then he could sleep on the davenport, Mom said. Lois wanted to go to the library in the evening, but Mom said she had to go out and get something for the baby's formula. Dad wondered if the baby would keep on crying all night. Everything seemed all mixed up.

A little baby coming into a home often upsets things for a while. But then things quiet down. A schedule and a routine are found, and the family begins to enjoy this great gift from God, a little child.

Dear God, help us to be patient when things are upset.

Taking care of babies can be tiring. Do you know a baby you could take care of for an afternoon or evening to give the parents some time off?

■ A SWAMP OR A RIVER?

Jer. 10:6-10: "But you, Lord, are the true God, you are the living God and the eternal king" (v. 10).

Dad," Tim said when he came home from school, "our teacher says all religions worship the same God, it's just that they have different names."

"Well, now," Dad said, "I don't know how that can be right. Hindus have more than one god, and none of the Hindu gods is more than an unusual human being. And Buddha himself didn't believe in a personal God.

"No, Tim," he concluded, "to accept all religions as equally true is to become a swamp. A river has banks and flows within those banks, and its waters give life. A swamp spreads all over because it has no banks and embraces everything. It becomes stagnant and sour, and instead of giving life it breeds death. The Bible teaches there is one way for us to be made acceptable to God, and that is through Christ."

Dear God, we thank you for the Bible which teaches us about you.

Choose a special missionary project for your family to give a gift to at Christmas. Begin to save for it now. Put out a jar or box labeled, "Our Christmas gift to missions."

■ DOES GOD KNOW ALL ABOUT ME?

Matt. 10:26-31: "even the hairs of your head have all been counted" (v. 30).

Lois was brushing her cat's fur. The brush was getting full of hair.

"Do you suppose God keeps count of cats' hair like he does ours?" she asked. "If he does, he's sure been busy the last few minutes."

Mom laughed.

"I don't know," she said. "God is different from us, Lois. I think the phrase, 'even the hairs of your head have all been counted' means God knows all about us."

"That's both good and bad," said Lois. "I don't like God to know about all my sins."

"Why not?" Mom asked. "He stands ready to forgive them because of what Jesus has done. When we believe that, we don't have to be afraid of God knowing all our sins."

"I guess not," Lois said thoughtfully, and then she added, "That makes me feel better."

You see all our sins, God. But you are willing to forgive us. We thank you.

Spend a few moments in silent reflection as each family member thinks of a sin that has been troubling him or her. Pray together that God will forgive these sins and bring healing.

■ WHO SHARES YOUR BATHTUB?

Rom. 14:7-9: "None of us lives for himself only" (v. 7).

Dad," Tim said, "I just saw a TV special on India. It showed people in a boat on the Benares River. In one end a man was holding out his pole, fishing. At the other end a little kid was leaning over the edge, going potty. And in the middle an old lady was brushing her teeth and scooping up water to rinse out her mouth."

"Pretty bad," Dad admitted. "But you know, Tim, with the movement of water around the world, we all share one big bathtub. And because of that, things like the dumping of radioactive wastes become world problems. We can't confine them to one area. Everything enters a single worldwide pool."

"I hadn't thought of that before," Tim said thoughtfully. "So what I do may affect lots of people."

"Right," said Dad. "The apostle Paul said none of us lives for himself only or dies for himself only. He meant that even though we'd like to be, none of us is his own boss. We all belong to each other. That's why we're safest when we try to do things God's way all the time. Loving God most of all and our neighbors as ourselves would prevent most problems and solve many others."

 We're nearsighted, Lord. We see only ourselves and those closest to us. Touch our eyes and give us perfect vision to see all, both near and far.

Some vacation day visit a water purification plant or a nuclear plant.

■ DON'T GIVE UP

Gal. 6:7-10: "So let us not become tired of doing good; for if we do not give up, the time will come when we will reap the harvest" (v. 9).

Mom was feeling discouraged. She loved her family very much and enjoyed doing her part to care for them and help them. But sometimes she wondered if they really appreciated what she did. They didn't thank her very often for all her work, and they seemed to take her for granted.

One day Mom was feeling particularly tired and discouraged, so she decided to pray about it. She shared her feelings openly with God for several minutes and asked for guidance. When she was finished she sensed the need to say something to her husband when he came home.

That night Mom and Dad had a long talk. Mom explained her feelings to Dad, and Dad apologized for not being more appreciative of all her work. He had let himself become wrapped up in problems at his job. Together they prayed that God would help them be more supportive of each other.

After that Dad made it a point to thank Mom for her work and compliment her when the family was together. Soon Tim and Lois began to do the same. And Mom knew that she would not become tired of doing good things for them, for they really did care about her.

Dear God, forgive us for taking each other for granted and not supporting each other. Help us to turn to you and share our needs with each other.

Think of ways you can show appreciation for each other more often.

50

■ CONTROLLING ANGER

2 Cor. 12:19-20: "I am afraid that I will find
quarreling and jealousy, hot tempers and selfishness" (v. 20).

Mom was baby-sitting a neighbor's three-year-old
boy. He wanted to run with his roller skates on in the
house. Mom wouldn't let him. He laid down on
the floor and kicked with his heels and screamed.
Mom let him scream. After a while he stopped.

Then he dug out some magazines and started to
rip them apart. Mom brought him some other toys
and started to play with him. But as soon as she took
the magazines away, he screamed again. When
screaming didn't help, he held his breath until he
started to turn blue.

"Really," Mom said to Dad, "I'm beginning to think
he gets his way every time he screams. Think what
he'll be like to live with when he grows up!"

Tempers can be awful things, Lord. We need
your help to control them. Teach us how to turn
to you when we get angry, so you can drain
away our anger before we hurt others.

**Think of someone you have been angry with recently.
Apologize to them and find a better way to deal
with your disagreement.**

■ OUTER SPACE

Isa. 40:21-26: "Look up at the sky! Who created the stars you see?" (v. 26).

Tim was listening intently to a conversation Dad and a friend were having. Dad's friend was a physicist, and he was talking about astrophysics, the physics of outer space.

"It is my opinion," Tim heard him say, "that the earth is unique and quite probably the only planet supporting human life. I view the earth and the universe as created by God for humans. All of it is precision-planned. If the moon were a hundred thousand miles closer to the earth, for example, the gravitational pull on the tides would be so great that most of our land would be under water. And if the sun were another million miles away, our planet would be too dark and too cold."

"I've heard," Dad said, "that it's possible that sometime in the future several planets will line up in a unique way."

"True," the physicist said. "But I don't believe, as some predict, that the result would be earthquakes or the earth pulled out of orbit. I don't think the planets exert that much gravitational pull on the earth. One day history will end. We don't know when. But as God's children we can trust him and not be afraid."

Tim slipped outside and stood looking at the moon and stars.

"Oh, God, how great you are," he whispered.

♫ Sing "How Great Thou Art" or another hymn of praise.

Plan a family trip to a planetarium or observatory.

■ GOD'S HIDDEN TREASURES

Psalm 104: "Lord, you have made so many things! How wisely you made them all!" (v. 24)

Dad!" Tim's voice was excited. "They think they've discovered a new source of oil off the Atlantic Coast! It could yield from 2 to 15 billion barrels!"

"That would be good news for all of us," Dad said. "I'm sure God has hidden many stores of usable materials if we can only find them."

"They think this supply lies 60 or 70 miles off the coast and is 6000 feet under the water. Can they dig that deep, Dad?"

"Yes, I think so, son. God's creation is really wonderful—the universe, our planet earth. And most wonderful of all are human beings whom God has given curious minds to explore things and creative abilities to solve problems. I never cease to wonder at it all. Only our selfishness spoils it. That is why, Tim, if this new source of oil comes through, we must pray that we might be wiser and less selfish in our use of what we discover."

O God, we marvel at your wonderful creation. Even more we marvel that, great as you are, you still care about each one of us individually. Help us to develop our gifts to the fullest extent.

Plan a family outing that will help you focus on God's creation.

■ UPSIDE DOWN ANSWERS TO PRAYER

2 Cor. 12:7-10: "My grace is all you need, for my power is strongest when you are weak" (v. 9).

All the children in Lois' church school class had been praying that Ann's eye operation would be successful. But when the doctors took off the bandages, Ann couldn't see a thing.

"I feel terrible," Lois said.

"Why don't we go and visit her?" Mom said. "We can bring her a new record."

Ann was cheerful. She squeezed Lois' hand. Lois was having trouble not crying, and a tear splashed down on Ann's hand.

"Don't feel bad," Ann said. "I still have arms and legs and a strong body, and ears and a nose, and a tongue, and a good brain, and Mom and Dad to help me. And other friends like you."

"God is answering your prayers," Mom said to Lois on the way home, "although in a different way than you thought. God is giving Ann much courage. Keep on praying for her every day. To have her so cheerful is almost a greater miracle than if she could see with her eyes."

Dear Jesus, we thank you that you never, never forsake us.

Are there any blind children you know to whom you can be a friend?

■ DISAGREEING AGREEABLY

Matt. 7:1-5: "Do not judge others, so that God will not judge you" (v. 1).

Mother's two old uncles, Henry and George, were visiting the Simons. They both liked to argue. Lois could hear their voices as she lay in bed.

"I say, George, how can you be a Christian, smoking as you do?"

George's voice boomed back, "Well, anyone who eats as much as you should talk! Reminds me of that joke. The old man asked his missus, 'Have you seen my belt around the house?' 'Oh,' his missus said, 'so it's gotten that big now, has it?' " Uncle George guffawed.

"Do they always quarrel?" Lois asked her mother the next day.

"They make up," Mom said. "They're out walking now."

"But you should have heard what they said to each other," Lois said.

"I know," Mom said. "We should never judge each other. All of us are different, and we have different ideas. It's alright to disagree. We have to learn to accept each other even when we disagree. I think that's really what Uncle Henry and Uncle George are trying to do."

Dear God, sometimes we argue with each other. When we do, help us to love, accept, and respect each other.

Discuss what your family disagrees about.
How do you settle disagreements?

■ LOST AND FOUND

Luke 15:1-7: "I am so happy I found my lost sheep. Let us celebrate!" (v. 6).

The Simons, the Duncans, and Brian's folks all decided to go to the park together to watch the Fourth of July fireworks. There were so many cars they had to park blocks away and walk. Lois was walking behind everybody else, bouncing a ball she had found. She came to a crosswalk, and suddenly realized she was no longer with the rest. People were thronging past, crisscrossing the street, but there was no Mom or Dad or Tim or the Duncans or Brian's family in sight. Lois felt like crying.

A police officer was standing in the center of the street, now and then blowing his whistle to let a car pass. He noticed Lois and walked over to her.

"I'm lost," Lois said, and then she started crying.

The officer said to her, "Come along, we'll find your family easy enough." They walked to an information booth and asked for her parents on the public address system.

"You left your work to take care of me," Lois said to the officer when he was going to leave.

"Helping lost people is the most important work we have," he said.

"That's the way Jesus feels too," Lois' mother said later. "Jesus said if he knew one sheep was lost, he would go and look and look for it till he found it. Jesus loves us so much."

 Thank you, Jesus, that you care for us always.

Think of times when you have felt lost and alone, either physically or spiritually. Spend some time talking about what it means to be found by Christ.

■ DON'T BEAR A GRUDGE

Lev. 19:17-18:   "Do not bear a grudge" (v. 17).

The Simons had just moved. Mom and Dad were busy telling the movers where to put the furniture. Tim and Lois were sitting on the curb, looking over the neighborhood. A rather pudgy boy kept riding past on a bicycle, staring at them. Finally he called out to Tim, "My little sister could beat your sister!"

For some reason this struck Tim funny, and he began to laugh. The boy rode by a second time, called out the same thing, and Tim laughed again. The boy screeched on the brakes, jumped off, and ran over to Tim.

"Why are you laughing at me?" he growled. He pushed Tim over and hit him as hard as he could. Then he jumped on his bike and rode away.

A couple of weeks later the boy's mother came over to talk with Tim's mother. That night at prayer time Mom said, "Just a couple of days before Roger hit you, Tim, his dad had walked out on the family and left them. Roger was upset and angry. I think we should begin praying for Roger and his family and start thinking about what we can do to help them."

"Yeah, I guess we should. It must be tough to have your dad leave you."

 Dear God, when people hurt us, help us to understand them and show us how we can love them.

Find a picture of Christ's crucifixion and put it up somewhere to remind you how Jesus forgave those who hated him.

■ A NEW CHURCH HOME

Matt. 25:31-46: "I was a stranger and you received me" (v. 35).

Hurry," Mom called to Tim and Lois, "we'll be late to church school."

"We're not going," Tim said.

Mom's mouth dropped open.

"We don't know anybody," Tim explained.

"Dad and I don't either," Mom said.

"But Tim and I have to go to classes alone," Lois said. "That's different."

"Mmm," Mom said. "Well, suppose we all just go to church today?" Dad nodded in agreement.

The next Wednesday evening the doorbell rang. Outside stood a whole family.

"We saw you in church Sunday," the man said. "We're the Duncans. I'm Harry. This is my wife, Martha, our daughter, June, and son, John. The pastor said you were new to our area."

Soon Tim was showing John his electric train, and Lois was asking June if they had a softball team she could join. When it was time for the Duncans to leave, John said, "Hey, you two, why don't you go with us to church school on Sunday? We could pick them up, couldn't we?" he asked his dad. His father nodded.

When the door closed on the Duncans, Tim said, "I can hardly wait till Sunday."

Help us to be kind to new neighbors and visitors who come to church.

Do you know of a new family in your church? Can you visit them?

■ WHAT'S WORRYING YOU?

Psalm 23: "Even if I go through the deepest darkness, I will not be afraid, Lord, for you are with me. Your shepherd's rod and staff protect me" (v. 4).

Tim was home late from school again. Mom had to help him fold papers for delivery.

"I can't understand why it takes you half an hour to walk home," she complained.

Tim said nothing.

"He's afraid," Lois piped up. "There are some big kids at school that like to wait for the little kids and beat them up. Tim goes 'way around so he won't run into them."

"So!" said Mom. "Now I understand. If you had only told me, I wouldn't have scolded you, Tim. I'm sorry the boys are so mean," she went on, "but if you stay out of their way for a while they'll probably get tired and give up. And if they don't, we'll do something about it. Tim," she concluded, "I hope you'll always feel free to tell Dad and me about things that are troubling you. Sometimes kids hesitate because they think their parents are too busy. That just isn't true. We want to help you and God wants to help you. You can feel free to tell us anything and everything."

Dear Jesus, thank you for being a friend who always stands ready to help.

Share a time when Jesus helped you. Is there any special worry you want to tell Jesus about now?

■ WHY CAN'T I EAT WHAT I WANT?

Dan. 1:8-16: "When the time was up, they looked healthier and stronger than all those who had been eating the royal food" (v. 15).

Tim scowled at the snacks on the counter: celery sticks stuffed with peanut butter and chopped dates; herbed whole wheat bread cubes toasted in the oven; dried apple chips and raisins; apples; lowfat milk.

"Why can't we ever have candy bars?" he complained. "Or corn chips and cola? At Brian's house they always have good snacks."

"Tim, you know very well that junk food doesn't do a thing for your body," Mom said. "Gobble it down fast, lots of calories, but few nutrients. Many years ago, Tim, a young man by the name of Daniel was living in a king's palace. He could have had all the rich pastries, sauces, and liquor he wanted. But he said no. He told them he would eat simple, nutritious food, and he would be healthier than all of them. And he was.

"God wants us to take care of our bodies. Doctors tell us to eat only as many calories as we burn, more whole grains and cereals, less sugar and fat, especially animal fat, and to watch the cholesterol and sodium. The eating habits you form now may stay with you for life. I want you to be healthy."

Dear God, teach us to take good care of our bodies.

Two cookbooks worth purchasing: the *American Heart Association Cookbook* (McKay, 1975), and the *More-With-Less* cookbook (Herald Press, 1976).

■ IT'S GOOD TO BE ALIVE

Psalm 116: "What can I offer the Lord for all his goodness to me?" (v. 12).

The Simons were eating Sunday dinner. They were talking about the Nortons, whose 10-year-old daughter had been killed in an automobile accident. The Nortons had given a large gift to a Bible college in memory of their daughter.

"Why don't we do the same?" Dad asked unexpectedly.

Lois looked startled. "But I'm not dead!" she protested.

"I know," Dad said quietly. "That's why I'm so thankful."

Dear God, teach us to be thankful for the many things we often take for granted.

Choose a song of praise and thanksgiving and sing it.

■ PUTTING GOD FIRST

Mal. 3:6-12: "Bring the full amount of your tithes" (v. 10).

The man from the newspaper office had just come and gone over accounts with Tim. After he left, Tim said, "Look, Mom! My first paycheck!"

"That's great," Mom said. "Have you thought of giving God a gift from it?"

Tim was feeling both happy and rich, so he said, "Sure! How much?"

"Dad and I always give ten percent of our earnings to the Lord," Mom said. "That custom began back in Old Testament times when God asked his people to bring the first of everything to him: the first grain harvested, the first apples from the orchard, the first vegetables from the garden. These gifts were then used to take care of the priests. God wanted his people to do this so they would always remember to put him first in their lives."

Tim had been figuring.

"Here," he said, holding out some money in his hand. "This will be for God. I want him to be first in my life."

Dear Lord, whatever we give to you came from you in the first place, and we can only thank you.

Does your family tithe? If you don't, why not begin now and experience the joy that comes from putting God first in this way?

■ WHO'S AFRAID OF THUNDER?

Mark 4:35-41: "Why are you frightened? Do you still have no faith?" (v. 40).

White lightning lit up Lois' room and then a giant clap of thunder crashed and rattled the windows. Rain poured down. Lois leaped from her bed, ran into her parents' room, dived into bed between them and lay there shivering and shaking. Mother reached over and put her arms around Lois. Lightning bathed the room in eerie whiteness again. Lois pulled the blanket over her head.

The next evening when Dad read the story of Jesus stilling the storm at sea, Lois asked, "If we had had more faith last night and had prayed, would Jesus have stilled that storm?"

"So you wouldn't have been so scared?" Dad asked. "Probably not for that reason, for God wants us to be courageous even when we are scared."

"When it storms," Mom said, "I imagine the wind and clouds and trees all crying out and saying, 'We hurt so much! When humans sinned, we felt the effects too. We long for the day when our world too will be in harmony again.'"

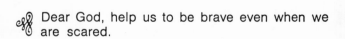 Dear God, help us to be brave even when we are scared.

Find a picture of Jesus and his disciples in the boat. Talk about how the different disciples may have felt and what they might have said. How was it that Jesus could sleep when it was storming?

■ DON'T JUST LIE THERE

2 Cor. 4:7-12: "though badly hurt at times, we are not destroyed" (v. 9).

Tim and Lois were visiting Grandpa and Grandma Johnson. Nancy, their cousin, was with them too. Grandpa and Grandma lived in a big old house that had a high veranda in front with a railing. Nancy was walking along the outside of the railing without hanging on to anything when she fell into the rosebushes below.

"Ouch, ouch, ouch!" she yelled, but she just laid there.

"Well," Lois said, "pick yourself up and get out."

Sometimes we get ourselves into trouble. Because the Christian life is a battle against sin, we fall into temptations and do what is wrong. But it doesn't do any good to just lie there and feel sorry for ourselves. We have to get up, straighten out what is wrong, and start over. God is with us to help us in every way, and he gives us power as we obey him and do what is right. The important thing is not to give up. We are perplexed, the apostle Paul says, because we don't know why things happen as they do, but we don't give up and quit.

Dear God, forgive us when we don't want to be rid of our sinful habits or when we get discouraged and want to give up just because living the Christian life isn't easy.

Discuss what sins are hard to give up. What makes us discouraged?

■ HAVE YOU EVER BEEN FOOLED?

Josh. 9:13-16:   "they decided to deceive him" (v. 4).

Tim was disgusted. He had taken the money he had earned delivering newspapers and had bought his mother a vegetable slicing gadget for Mother's Day. But it didn't work. On TV the potato slices rolled off easily, even and perfect. The carrots were sliced into thin little sticks. And it was so fast and easy. But when Tim's mother tried to use it, it wouldn't stick to the counter top. The potatoes came out crooked, and the whole thing kept falling apart. Plus it was hard to wash. Tim was mad. He felt cheated and deceived.

"TV has some good programs but it also tells lies," his father said that night at the dinner table. "We need to learn to listen with questioning minds and not believe everything. People have practiced deception since the beginning of time. God does not want us to be fooled or tricked. No matter how convincing something appears to be, we must not rely only on our own judgment and common sense but trust God to give us wisdom and insight."

Dear God, make us aware of the times when people try to deceive us in one way or another.

When you watch TV next, see if you can find examples of half-truths and deception.

■ EVEN OUR BLACKEST SIN

Psalm 51: "Wash away all my evil and make me clean from my sin!" (v. 2).

Let me tell you the story behind this beautiful prayer of confession," Dad said after he had read Psalm 51 to the family.

"King David was very popular. The people loved and idolized him. But all this hero worship gave him a big head, and he thought he had a right to anything he wanted.

"One of the officers in David's army was named Uriah. Uriah had a pretty wife, and David wanted her for himself. He brought her to his palace while Uriah was away fighting, and David slept with her. Later she told him she was pregnant. Then David sent a messenger to his general, ordering him to put Uriah in the front lines and allow him to be killed. That way David could get rid of Uriah and marry Bathsheba."

"How awful!" Lois exclaimed. "What happened?"

"Uriah was killed in battle, and David married Bathsheba. But God sent Nathan the prophet to rebuke him. David repented of his terrible sin, and God forgave him. But the evil consequences of his actions could not be changed. We human beings are capable of horrible sins, but how amazing and wonderful it is that God still forgives us if we repent and ask him for mercy."

 Dear God, cleanse us from all our sins, from selfishness, pride, and greed. Keep us from using people to get what we want.

Discuss ways parents and children sometimes use each other. In what ways can you be more loving in your family?

■ THE STUPENDOUS SHAKE

1 Thess. 4:13-18: "And so we will always be with the Lord" (v. 17).

Tim and Lois found a bird that had flown into the side of the house and broken a wing. It was lying on the ground.

"I wonder if it is hurt inside," Lois said.

They brought the bird in the house, lined a shoe box with soft grass and leaves and laid the bird in it. They chopped bread and peanuts and tried to feed the bird and gave it water to drink from an eye dropper. But in the night it died.

"Oh, well," Tim said, "let's have a funeral."

Mom watched them as they dug a hole in the backyard. Just before Tim put the cover on the box to bury it, he shook the box. The bird didn't move. Tim sighed. "Guess it's really dead," he said.

"Children," Mom said after they had buried the bird, "when we die, our bodies too will become still. People could shake us, but like the bird, we too won't feel it. But then the resurrection day will come. And when Jesus comes and shakes us, do you know what will happen? Our bodies will stir and get new life, and we will be raised with brand-new bodies to live with God forever."

 Dear God, thank you that we can look forward to having new, perfect bodies and a life with you forever.

Find a picture of Jesus and the resurrection and hang it up to remind you of our Christian hope.

■ RAIN, RAIN, RAIN

2 Cor. 9:6-15: "And God is able to give you more than you need, so that you will always have all you need for yourselves and more than enough for every good cause" (v. 8).

Tim and Lois were visiting their Uncle Carl who lived on a farm. It had rained and rained. Uncle Carl couldn't cut the hay or bring it into the barn, and the corn wasn't growing, because it needed sun. But Uncle Carl remained cheerful.

"You don't complain," Lois said. "People in the city complain if it rains just a little bit, and it spoils their weekend plans. But when it rains here, you can't even get your work done. And still you don't complain."

Uncle Carl smiled.

"You forget," he said, "I've had years of training. A farmer always struggles with the weather. It seems it either rains too much or not enough. But in the end it all works out. And if one year is really bad, and we don't get good crops, usually we make up for it the next year. God takes care of us. Maybe that's why I feel so close to God, because I'm so dependent on him. And he has never failed yet. He provides enough for us, and not only for us," Uncle Carl smiled even more, "but through our work, he provides for all of you in the city too."

 Dear God, we thank you for sun and rain, for seeds, and for farmers who work so we will have enough to eat.

Discuss where the food you ate for dinner came from. What problems do you think the farmers might have had in producing it?

■ DON'T FORGET THE BACK ROWS!

Matt. 14:13-21: "You yourselves give them something to eat!" (v. 16)

Let's try to imagine what it was like that day Jesus
fed the five thousand," Mom said after Tim had
finished reading the Bible passage for the evening.
"Jesus gave the baskets to the disciples and ordered
them to distribute the food to the people who were
sitting in lines. But suppose that the disciples took the
baskets and all of them began to walk up and down
the first three rows. Then suppose Andrew asked,
'Shouldn't some of us move to the back?' The others
said, 'Oh, but we're not through here yet. People are
still holding out their hands.' But Andrew insisted,
so at last the others said, 'OK, you go, but we're
busy here.'

"Andrew moved to the back, but soon he ran out of
bread and fish. He ran back to the other disciples.
'I need more food,' he said, 'and someone to help me.
There are so many hungry people back there.' 'You
want *more* food?' the disciples asked. 'We gave you
some. Do you want us to give it all away? And you
want us to leave our work here? Why, these people
are closest to us. Aren't they our first responsibility?' "

Lord, help us to care about those who are
hungry.

**Go without dinner one night and give that money
for world hunger relief.**

69

■ BREAKFAST WITH JESUS

John 21:1-14:   "Come and eat" (v. 12).

Did Jesus have skin when he arose from the dead?"
Lois asked.

"He must have," Mom said, "because we read that
he asked Thomas to touch him to see that he was real.
And he cooked breakfast for his disciples one morning
after they had been fishing all night and were tired."

"I like the way Jesus loves people," Lois said. "He
cares for them by feeding them when they're hungry
and doing all those ordinary things—not just doing
miracles all the time."

"That makes it easier for us to follow his example,
doesn't it?" Mom said.

Help us, Lord, to show our love to people in
everyday ways.

If possible, arrange as a family to go to the beach,
a lake, or a river early some morning to have
breakfast. Broiling fish over an open fire would be
especially meaningful. Or you can split wieners, put
cheese between, wrap bacon around, broil over an
open fire, and then put them between buns. Or take a
simple breakfast along. Read the devotion after
you've had breakfast. Or, find out the birth date of
some older person who lives alone. Call and ask
if your family can bring breakfast to him or her.

■ TIPSY

Eph. 5:15-20: "Do not get drunk with wine, which will only ruin you; instead, be filled with the Spirit" (v. 18).

The ringing of the telephone awakened Mrs. Simon.

"Tim? Is that you, Tim? I couldn't recognize your voice. Come over to Brian's house and get you? You're sick? What's wrong? You're too sick to tell me? We'll be right over."

Mom and Dad put on their clothes and left the house. It was the beginning of a week's vacation for Tim, and he had gone to Brian's to spend the night.

Mom found both Brian and Tim in the bathroom. They were sitting on the floor, and their clothes smelled of vomit.

"What in the world . . . ?" Mom began. Then she saw Dad come down the hall with some empty beer cans in his hands. "Look what I found in the kitchen," he said.

"Where are your folks?" Dad asked Brian.

"Visiting friends for the weekend," he said.

"Where did you two get the beer?" Mom asked.

"From the refrigerator," Brian said. "My parents drink it all the time."

"We wanted to see who could drink the most," Tim said sheepishly. "I wouldn't have had *any* if I had known it makes you so sick."

 Dear God, help us to find true excitement and joy in you and not in alcohol or drugs. Teach us to be good stewards of our bodies.

Talk about the dangers of alcoholism and drug addiction.

■ A CRUEL MASTER

Titus 2:1-8: "be sober, sensible, and self-controlled" (v. 2).

T im," Dad said the next evening, "there's a lot you should understand about alcohol. One of the biggest health and safety problems in our country is alcoholism —becoming addicted to drinking. Alcoholics have to drink more and more all the time because their bodies demand it. And at the same time their bodies are being affected. Their kidneys or livers may suffer. They may be unable to work properly. They may become irritable or unable to concentrate.

"When things get really bad, alcoholics may start to tremble or shake. They may have 'blackouts,' which means they may not remember anything for long periods of time. Alcoholics sometimes beat other people, even people they love, without even remembering it.

"Now why some people become slaves to alcohol and others can drink occasionally without losing control, doctors don't really know. But you *can* get hooked on alcohol just as you can get hooked on drugs. If people never drank excessively it would help. But even then alcohol would still become the cruel master of some.

"I don't know about you, Tim, but I don't want alcohol to be my master. I like to be free."

Dear God, help us to live in such a way that we will be free and responsible people, in control of ourselves.

Do you know someone who has overcome their dependence on alcohol and who would be willing to talk with you about it?

■ THE JOY OF TREE HOUSES

Matt. 14:22-33: "he went up a hill by himself to pray" (v. 23).

Tim sat in his tree house, all alone among the boughs of the tree. He listened to the birds sing and the leaves whisper. It felt so good just to be all alone. He sat there and thought and thought.

The smell of Mom baking chocolate-chip cookies finally brought him down.

"Why do I like being alone sometimes?" he asked Mom as he munched on some of her cookies.

"We all need times to be alone," Mom said. "It's good to be alone once in awhile. Then we can shut out other people's voices and ideas and think. We can think about God and how much he loves us, and what he wants to do for us and what he wants to do with our lives. We can become quiet inside. And we can pray. Jesus felt the need to be alone. Sometimes he would spend several hours alone talking with his Father. If Jesus felt the need for this, we should too."

Dear Father, thank you for times when we can be alone with you.

Does every member of your family have opportunities to be alone? If they don't, what can be done to make this possible?

■ A GENTLE TONGUE

Eph. 5:1-5: "Your life must be controlled by love, just as Christ loved us and gave his life for us" (v. 2).

Get off the phone so I can call!" yelled Tim, grabbing the phone away from Lois.

"Hey! Don't do that!" cried Lois. She hit Tim on his head and arm till he dropped the phone.

Tim started to kick Lois, but he threw himself off balance and fell on the floor. Lois burst out laughing. Just then Mom walked in the kitchen.

"Make her hang up," Tim screamed.

Lois covered the phone with her hand and hissed, "Shut up!"

"All right!" Mom said.

Lois caught the look in her mother's eye. "I have to go," she said hurriedly to her friend on the phone.

"Love is *kind*," Mom said when Lois hung up.

"Well, it wasn't kind of Lois to stay on the phone so long," Tim complained.

"No," Mom said, "and neither of you were kind in the way you talked to each other. I don't want to hear that kind of talk again for a long time!"

Dear God, help us to be kind when we talk to each other.

Each time you say something unkind, write an IOU to the person involved and promise to do them a favor.

74

■ GIVE EVERYONE A CHANCE

1 Thess. 5:8-11: "encourage one another and help one another" (v. 11).

Mom and Dad were having a big discussion. Dad was thinking of taking some classes to earn another degree. If he got it he might get some better job offers. But Mom had surprised him by saying she would like to go back to school, too. She wanted to become a hospital chaplain. They talked for a long time. Finally Dad said, "I think it's your turn to study and have a chance to see some of your dreams come true."

"It will mean changes," Mom warned. "Things will be different around here, and I'll need lots of help and support. I won't be able to do some of the things that I'm doing now."

The Simons talked about some of the things that would change if Mom went back to school. Then Lois said, "I still think it's a good idea! Let's all help out." Together they began to plan how they would help Mom attend classes and earn another degree.

The happiest families are those where the good of every member is sought, where all family members work together to fulfill some dreams that each person has. To encourage and help each other is Jesus' way for us.

 Dear God, teach us to love our family members as much as we love ourselves. Help us to find more ways to encourage and help them.

Ask each other what some of your personal dreams are. What can you do to help more of those dreams come true?

■ TRUSTING GOD

Isa. 41:8-10: "I will protect you and save you" (v. 10).

Lois and Tim's little cousin Martha and her mother were visiting them. Martha was just learning to walk.

"Here, hold my hand," Tim said, but Martha kept dropping Tim's hand and sitting down. Plop!

"Try standing behind Martha and holding both her hands," Mom suggested.

Tim did, and when Martha started to wobble, he steadied her. Soon she was walking across the room.

"When we try to hang on to Jesus," Mom said, "when we try to be good just by ourselves, without trusting God, we stumble and fall. But when we trust God to take care of us, it goes much better. Then he steadies us and holds us up when we start to fall. He is right there to help us."

Thank you, Jesus, that you are willing to hold our hand and take care of us.

Find a picture of Jesus, the Good Shepherd, and put it on the bulletin board to remind you that Jesus will lead you.

■ WHAT'S WRONG WITH SWEARING?

Matt. 5:33-37: ''Just say 'Yes' or 'No'—anything else you say comes from the Evil One'' (v. 37).

Tim was mad. He threw his baseball glove on the floor and said something that made his mother look up.

"Tim!" Her voice was sharp. "We don't swear."

"Why not?" Tim was defiant. "Everybody does."

"We don't swear," Mom said firmly. "God has commanded us not to. We are not to take the name of the Lord in vain. That means we do not use God's name thoughtlessly in cursing or swearing. Jesus said we should be so honest that when we say something, people will know it is true without our having to use God's name to prove we are telling the truth. Tim, God has forbidden us to swear, and because of that, we, in our home, just don't swear. And I don't want to hear you swearing."

Dear God, forgive us when we hurt you by using your name carelessly.

Talk about your family's habits in regard to swearing.

■ A PERSONALLY GUIDED TOUR

John 14:1-7: "I am the way, the truth, and the life" (v. 6).

The Simons had gone to visit Grandpa and Grandma Simon who lived 2000 miles away. It had been years since Dad had been there. The city had grown, and Grandpa and Grandma had moved to a different place.

"I guess I'm lost," Dad confessed.

"Oh, dear!" Mom said.

It was almost midnight, and Tim and Lois, who had fallen asleep in the car, woke up.

"There aren't any gas stations open; who can help us?" Mom said.

Just then they saw a man come out of an apartment building and start toward his car. Quickly Dad pulled alongside and asked where 1916 Oak Street was.

"You new here?" the man asked.

"Not really strangers," Lois piped up. "It's just that we've been gone so long."

The man smiled. "Follow me," he said. "I'll lead you."

Getting in his car, he drove off and led the way.

As the Simons followed him, Dad said, "This is what Jesus meant when he said 'I am the way.' Jesus not only gives us directions; he goes with us and shows us the way, so we're sure not to get lost."

Thank you, Jesus, that you will be with us all through life to show us the way.

Talk about the different ways God guides us.

■ MAKING MEALTIMES HAPPY

1 Cor. 11:17-34: "each one goes ahead with his own meal" (v. 21).

Would you mind passing the meat to me please?" Mom asked.

Lois, Tim, and Dad all sat with their heads bent over their plates, intent on their own concerns. Tim and Dad were talking about the day's baseball scores. Lois was daydreaming.

"Pass me the meat please," Mom tried again.

Still no response.

"Really!" Mom said, getting up and going over to get the meat.

"Oh, oh, sorry!" Dad said.

"I think," Mom said, "we need to talk about how to make mealtimes happier."

Here are some guidelines the Simon family adopted:
1. Begin with a prayer of thanksgiving.
2. Be aware of the needs of others.
3. Don't interrupt each other.
4. Say "please" and "thank you."
5. Don't use mealtime for scolding or lectures.
6. Don't combine TV viewing, especially the news, with eating.

Dear God, we have so much to learn about being considerate of each other. Teach us.

Next mealtime try to follow the suggestions above.

■ CHEER-UP PARTIES

Phil. 4:10-20: "it is a great joy to me that . . . you once more had the chance of showing that you care for me" (v. 10).

Tim, Lois, and Mom were having a conference. For weeks now Dad had looked tired, had chewed his pens, and had said little during mealtimes.

"He's worried," Mom explained. "They're laying off people at work. He's afraid he'll be next. I'm sure even if that happens, God will take care of us, but Dad feels the responsibility of providing for his family."

"What can we do?" Tim asked.

"I know!" Lois said. "Let's have a cheer-up party for Dad."

"How?" Tim asked.

"Well," Mom began, "I could make his favorite foods, homemade rolls and apple pie. We could use our best china, and candles."

"I'll make a poster," Lois said. "Something like, 'Who's the greatest? Our Dad!' "

"I guess I could clean the garage and mow the lawn," Tim said. "But it would be even more fun to give him a ticket to the baseball game."

Lois giggled. "And we could hug and kiss him, really fuss over him," she said. "This is going to be fun." Her eyes sparkled in anticipation.

Dear Lord, help us to notice when somebody is discouraged, so we can do something special for them.

Is there someone for whom you should have a cheer-up party?

■ THE BEST WAY TO FIGHT

Matt. 5:43-48: "love your enemies and pray for those who persecute you" (v. 44).

I hate Mrs. Conway!" Tim screamed, throwing his football in the corner. "Every time our ball goes in her yard, she yells."

"The arthritis in her hands has been bothering her a lot," Mom said. "You could wash her car for her."

"I could *whaat?*"

"Wash her car," Mom said evenly. "It's painful for her to have her hands in cold water."

"You gotta be kiddin'," Tim said.

The next Saturday morning Tim came from the garage carrying a pail and brush and rags.

"I really don't want to," he complained.

Mom just smiled.

An hour later he came back into the kitchen.

"Know what?" he said. "After I was all through, she told me I was a nice boy but she still doesn't like it when our football goes in her flower beds. Can you beat that?

"She did give me this, though," he said, digging a ten-dollar bill out of his pocket. "She said from the looks of it we could use a new football." Tim straightened out the bill. "I guess we could always play in the park. . . . I guess there'd be more room there too."

Thank you, God, that there are happy ways to settle quarrels.

Find a picture of people arguing. Why do you think they are arguing? How might they be able to settle their quarrel?

■ WILL THE WORLD END SOON?

Matt. 24:36-44: "No one knows, however, when that day and hour will come—neither the angels in heaven nor the Son; the Father alone knows" (v. 36).

Tim had spent the night with Jimmy. The next day at dinner he burst out with, "Dad, is the world going to end soon?"

"Why do you ask?" Dad wanted to know.

"Well, Jimmy and I went to this scary movie last night. It showed all sorts of things that are happening now, and the man kept saying it all proved that the world is going to end soon."

Dad stabbed some peas with his fork.

"When I was young, I saw a movie like that too," he said.

"You did?"

"Yes. You see, people have always wondered when the world would end. Life as we know it on this planet will someday cease to exist," Dad said. "But when, we don't know. The important thing is for us to be ready to meet God any time, and then carry on faithfully with the work he has given us to do."

Dear Jesus, help us look forward with joy to the time when we shall see you face to face.

Ask yourselves this question: If you knew for sure that Jesus would return tomorrow, is there anything special you would want to do today?

■ THROWAWAYS

Luke 9:10-17: "the disciples took up twelve baskets of what was left over" (v. 17).

W hat is this?" Mom asked, lifting out of the trash can a knit blouse that belonged to Lois.

"I don't like it," Lois said.

"We don't throw clothes away," Mom said.

"Why not?" asked Lois. "I can get more."

Mom sighed.

"We threw away the plastic glasses you used at your party last night," Lois said. "And every time we go on a picnic, we throw away the plates. I've seen you throw away food, too."

That night Mom and Dad had a long, long talk. Afterward they had a family conference.

"We *are* too wasteful," Dad said. "We talk of how God has made us managers of trees and oil and coal and food and money, but we don't always do what we know is right. Jesus had power to provide huge quantities of food for people. But even though he had plentiful resources, he didn't waste them. He had the disciples gather up the leftover pieces. I think we should learn from him. Let's discuss what we can do so we don't throw away so much."

Dear God, help us to be content with less and be truly thankful for what we have. Forgive us when we are fussy and spoiled.

Discuss how your family can stop throwing resources away and instead conserve them.

■ DON'T GET SHORTCHANGED

Gen. 41:53—42:2: "there is grain in Egypt" (42:2).

Do you remember the story of Joseph and his brothers?" Dad asked. "Joseph was his father's pet. This made his brothers jealous. Then, in a dream, God told Joseph that one day he would be so great all his brothers would fall at his feet. Joseph foolishly told his brothers about his dream. That made them even more disgusted.

"One day Joseph brought lunch to his brothers in the field. When they saw him, they said, 'Here's our chance to get even with this smart little kid.' So they threw him into a pit. They were so angry with him that when some Egyptian traders came along, they sold Joseph to them.

"Some years later," Dad continued, "famine struck. Joseph's brothers had nothing to eat. Only in Egypt, where Joseph now had risen to great authority, was there food. Joseph's brothers, of course, did not know what had happened to Joseph. All they knew was they needed food.

"Never pay back wrong for wrong," Dad concluded. "You will always get shortchanged. The happy ending to the story is that Joseph forgave his brothers and provided food for them. But this came only after years of suffering, bad consciences, and sorrow for all of them, including their father."

It's hard not to be mean to those who are mean to us. Help us, Father, when we are tempted.

Discuss what could have happened if, in the devotion on p. 57, Tim had not forgiven Roger.

■ SEAT BELTS

Prov. 6:20-23:   "their correction can teach you how to live" (v. 23).

The Simons were waiting for Dad to start the car.

"What're you waiting for, Dad?" Tim asked. "We're all here."

"I'm waiting for you to put on your seat belts," Dad said quietly.

"Seat belts are dumb," Tim said as he fumbled around for his.

Some days later the phone in Dad's office rang. Somebody had hit Mom's car while she was driving. She had some bruises and they had taken her to the hospital.

When Dad brought Mom home that night, Tim and Lois stood and stared at her black and blue marks and the cuts on her face.

"I had my seat belt on. Without it I would have gone through the windshield," Mom said.

After that Dad didn't have to tell Tim to put on his seat belt.

Life is the most precious gift God has given us. He expects us to take care of this gift and not to take risks that might destroy it.

Dear God, thank you for giving us life and protecting us from accidents. Help us to do our part too.

Talk about why we use seat belts.

■ WATER, WATER EVERYWHERE . . .

1 Cor. 4:1-5: "You should think of us as Christ's servants, who have been put in charge of God's secret truths. The one thing required of such a servant is that he be faithful to his master" (vv. 1-2).

A letter had come from the city water department. If there was going to be enough water to last through the summer, people would have to conserve, the notice declared.

"We'll have to be good stewards," Dad said.

"What does *steward* mean?" Lois asked.

"Stewards," Dad said, "were managers. They often were given money or food and drink to distribute wisely. God has given us this earth and all its resources to manage wisely and justly. For example, if we were really good stewards, there would be no hunger in the world. As it is now, some of us have far more than we need, and so some do not have enough. Water is a precious resource too. If we waste it, all of us will suffer."

Dear God, sometimes we are like children reaching in a cookie jar. We grab fistfuls and gobble them down. Loosen our tight grip. Control our appetites. Teach us to share, so all will have enough.

Discuss ways your family can conserve on water. After a week, report what each one has done.

■ HOW GOD FORGIVES

Psalm 32: "Happy are those whose sins are forgiven" (v. 1).

Lois was crying. She had been at the variety store with her friend Becky, and she had seen a pretty hair barrette. But it cost more money than Lois had. When Becky went to the checkout counter with her notebook paper, Lois strolled back to where the barrette was. She looked around and then quickly slipped it up the sleeve of her sweater. But as she walked out, the swinging door hit her sleeve and the barrette fell to the floor. The checker grabbed Lois and called her mother. Mom had come to get her, and after talking with the store manager she brought Lois home.

The store manager, Mom said, would not report it to the police. But had Lois thought how she had hurt Jesus? Lois cried even more.

Finally Lois and her Mom got down on their knees. Lois asked God to forgive her. When they got up, Mom put her arms around Lois and kissed her.

"When we confess our sins, God forgives and forgets," she said. "It is as though he throws them in the deep, deep sea, and then, as Corrie ten Boom has said, puts up a sign that says, 'No fishing allowed.'"

"Honest?" Lois was smiling through her tears. "Mom," she said, hugging her, "I never, never want to steal again."

Thank you, God, that you forgive our sins and then forget them.

Is there some sin God has been reminding you of that you should confess and receive forgiveness for?

■ WHO WILL DO THE DIRTY WORK?

John 13:1-7: "You call me Teacher and Lord, and it is right that you do so, because that is what I am. I, your Lord and Teacher, have just washed your feet. You, then, should wash one another's feet. I have set an example for you, so that you will do just what I have done for you" (vv. 13-15).

Tim," Mom said, "the trash cans need to be scrubbed."

"Yuck!" Tim said. "That's not for me!"

Mom was silent for a moment.

"You know," she said, "Jesus never thought he was above doing any task, no matter how dirty it was. He even washed his disciples' feet once."

"Why would he do that?" Tim asked with a puzzled look. "Couldn't they wash their own feet when they took baths?"

"In Jesus' day people wore sandals," she explained. "The roads were dusty, and people's feet got dirty. When they arrived at a house, the servants would take off the guests' sandals, wash their feet, and massage them with oil. Everyone knew that was servants' work. And yet Jesus was not only willing to do it, but he told his disciples he was doing it as an example for them. They were never to think of themselves so highly that they were unwilling to do unpleasant but necessary things to help people."

Tim was silent. Then he disappeared outside. A few minutes later Mom heard water running and the clanking of the trash cans.

Dear God, forgive us when we think we are too important to do little chores.

Try making it a practice to do little chores without being asked to do them.

■ HELPING MY CHURCH GROW

John 1:35-51: "Philip found Nathanael and told him, 'We have found the one whom Moses wrote about' " (v. 45).

Lois and Tim were excited. It was vacation church school time.

"I can't play ball mornings next week," Tim said to Brian. "I'll be going to VCS."

"What's that?"

Tim explained.

"School, huh? Doesn't sound very exciting to me."

"Oh, but it is! We have games, too." Then, as though he had just thought of it, Tim added, "Why don't you come?"

"How'd I get there?"

"You could ride with us."

"Hey, let's get Jimmy too," Brian said.

"OK, OK," Lois interrupted, "but leave some room in the car. I want to ask Ann and Mary."

That year at VCS both Lois and Tim's classes had extra members. Lois and Tim did what Jesus' first disciples did. When John and Andrew and Philip met Jesus, they went and told their friends. Lois and Tim brought their friends to church where they could learn more about Christ.

Lord, forgive us when we keep to ourselves the good things we learn about you.

Is there someone you can invite and bring along to church or church school?

■ WHEN TO RUN AWAY

Gen. 3:1-7: "the woman saw how beautiful the tree was" (v. 6).

Lois and her mother were out shopping when Mom stopped at the variety store.

"There's a sale on yard goods," Mom said. "Maybe we can find something for a summer dress for you."

Lois hadn't been in the store since the time she had been caught trying to steal the hair barrette. She was glad when she saw a new checker at the checkout counter.

Mom sat down to look at patterns. Lois started to wander around. At the jewelry counter she noticed a delicate gold wrist chain. She slipped it on. How pretty it was! Then suddenly Lois remembered the story of Eve which Mom had read to her. Eve had looked at the fruit which God had forbidden her to eat. It had looked so delicious that Eve's mouth had watered. She had reached out, picked it, and then eaten it.

Lois dropped the bracelet and hurried back to Mom. It was dangerous, she decided, to stand and look at something she wanted very much but couldn't afford. She wasn't going to let temptation get the best of her.

Dear God, help us to run from situations that are tempting us to do wrong, especially when we feel we are not strong enough to say no.

Memorize this verse: "Resist the devil, and he will run away from you" (James 4:7).

■ PEACEMAKERS

Matt. 5:1-12: "Happy are those who work for peace; God will call them his children!" (v. 9).

Tim and Lois were fighting. Tim had been watching a sports broadcast, but he had left the room during a commercial to get a snack. While he was gone Lois changed the channel and started watching a science special.

"Why did you change the channel?" Tim demanded.

"Because you watch sports all the time, and this special is only going to be on once."

"But I was watching the game!" Tim insisted.

"You've been watching the game for two hours. It's my turn," Lois said.

The argument got louder and louder. Finally Dad came in the room.

"If you two can't find a way to solve this argument, I know a simple way Mom and I can have some peace and quiet," Dad said sternly.

"What's that?" Tim asked.

"We'll just unplug the TV for the rest of the week. There's no sense in letting it disturb our family life."

"Oh," Tim said.

"I think Tim and I can work something out, Dad," Lois said.

Dear God, forgive us when we are selfish and fight with each other. Help us to work things out and be peacemakers.

Try using a "problem-solving" approach to disagreements in your family instead of just fighting over things.

■ ORANGE JUICE COMES FROM ORANGES

Gen. 1:1—2:4: "I have provided all kinds of grain and all kinds of fruit for you to eat" (1:29).

Lois and Tim's six-year-old cousin Nancy was visiting them. She stood watching Lois squeezing oranges for juice.

"Auntie, auntie!" she cried, as Lois' mother came in the kitchen. "Lois is getting orange juice from oranges."

Nancy had seen orange juice only in bottles or frozen in cans in the supermarket, and it had never occurred to her that orange juice came from oranges.

The next day the Simons took Nancy to an orange grove so she could pick oranges from a tree. They visited a nut grove too and showed her nuts on trees. They stopped at a produce ranch and walked among the rows of lettuce and cauliflower and cabbage. Finally they drove to a dairy and saw cows lined up in stalls. They watched people put milking machines on them. By the end of the day, Nancy's eyes were big.

"I sure learned a lot," she said.

"God made the earth so rich that we can get from it all the food we need," Mom said. "He loves us and cares for us in so many ways."

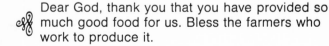
Dear God, thank you that you have provided so much good food for us. Bless the farmers who work to produce it.

If you live in the city and haven't done so, plan to visit a farm. If you live on a farm, perhaps through your church you could invite some city children to visit you.

■ ABRAHAM LAUGHED

Gen. 17:15-21:   "Abraham bowed down with his face touching the ground, but he began to laugh" (v. 17).

Tim's father had been reading the story of how God promised Abraham and Sarah a son. Through that son God eventually would bless the whole world. Abraham and Sarah waited and waited, but nothing happened. Finally, many years after Sarah was past the age of having a baby, God appeared to Abraham and told him again that they would have a son. Abraham laughed. Sarah laughed too. It was funny. Two people old enough to be a grandpa and grandma having a baby!

"What happened?" Lois asked.

"Sarah did have a baby," Dad said. "And guess what they called him: Isaac. *Isaac* means 'he laughs.' And Isaac became one of the ancestors of Jesus."

"God must like to handle tough assignments, huh?" Tim asked.

"Jesus said nothing was too hard for God," Dad said.

"Nothing?" Tim sat thinking. "Can God even help me control my temper?"

"I'm sure that would really please him," Dad said.

Tim laughed. "That would be somethin'," he said. "That would really be somethin'."

Dear God, forgive us for not trusting you to help us with hard situations in life. Increase our faith.

On a prayer card or in a prayer book, write something really difficult that you would like God to do for you, something you think would glorify him.

■ SOMETIMES IT'S BETTER TO LOSE

Gen. 27:1-45: "Perhaps . . . I will bring a curse on myself instead of a blessing" (v. 12).

W hew!" Lois said. "I had a close call at school today, but Jesus helped me."

"How?" Mom asked.

"We had this history test. I didn't know some of the answers, but I was sitting close to April. April always gets the answers right. It would've been real easy to have copied from April's paper. But then I remembered —you know—what happened at the store, and I said, 'No way! Help me, Lord!' and I put my hand up as a blinder for my eyes."

"How did the test go?"

"I don't know. But even if I don't get a good grade, I feel good inside."

Mom smiled. "Sometimes we win by losing," she said.

"That's for sure!" Lois said. "I know God forgives our sins, but I have a hard time forgiving them."

Mom smiled again. "You can always study harder and do better on the next test."

Lord Jesus, we are weak. Make us strong when we are tempted.

Talk about Jacob's act of deception with his father. What did he gain by receiving his brother's blessing? What did he lose?

■ IS THE WORLD ALL BAD?

Luke 10:25-37: "But a Samaritan who was traveling that way came upon the man, and when he saw him, his heart was filled with pity" (v. 33).

If all we knew about the world we live in was what we learned from TV, we might think it was falling apart, and everything and everybody was bad," Mom said. "But just think how many good and kind people there are too," she added.

"Remember how the people three blocks away brought back our dog when he ran away?" Tim said.

"I was standing in line at the supermarket this afternoon," Mom said, "when the lady in front said, 'You go first. You have just a few things. I have a whole cart full.'"

Lois also spoke up. "Remember how our neighbors came to stay with Tim and me when Dad went to get Mom after her car accident?"

"There's a lot of love and kindness and goodness in the world," Mom said. "We need to remember that. I suppose the wounded man who lay on the road to Jericho after the robbers had beat him up wondered if the world was all bad."

"Especially when the first two people who came by didn't even stop to help him," Tim remembered.

"But then the Samaritan came," Mom said. "And how generous and kind he was!"

Dear Father in heaven, help us, as we live on earth, to reflect your love by being kind and good to others.

Discuss good things that have happened to you.

■ "WE'RE GLAD YOU CAME TO VISIT US"

Gen. 18:1-8: "please do not pass by my home without stopping; I am here to serve you" (v. 3).

Lois and Tim's grandpa and grandma were coming for a visit.

"What can we do to make their visit a happy one?" Mom asked.

"Can we learn anything from this story?" Dad asked. He read the story of Abraham's heavenly visitors.

"Abraham went out to greet them," Mom said. "We can all go to the airport to meet grandpa and grandma's plane."

"Abraham brought water for their feet. We can ask them if they would like time to take showers," Lois said.

"We'll want to get a room ready for them," Mom said. "Fresh linens, clean curtains, towels laid out, a night light. And we should keep the bathroom clean."

"Abraham suggested they rest under the tree," Tim noted. "We shouldn't keep them up too late or wake them up by being loud."

"And we shouldn't plan so much for them to do that they get all tired," Dad added.

"It says," Tim pointed out, "Abraham served them himself when they ate. We should do the same, and watch to see if they need anything."

"Abraham was a good host, wasn't he?" asked Lois.

"We can be good hosts too!" Tim said.

Dear Lord, help us to be courteous and considerate of each other.

Discuss little courtesies that make life more pleasing for all of us.

■ WHEN WE ALL WORK TOGETHER

2 Cor. 8:13-15: "since you have plenty at this time, it is only fair that you should help those who are in need" (vv. 13-14).

Hurricane Edgar had hit the West Indies, the TV commentator said on the six o'clock news. Thousands were homeless. The TV screen showed little children sleeping under trees.

"I wish I could do something to help them," Tim said, "but I don't know how. And even if I did, what good can the little I am able to give do?"

"You are already helping them," Dad said quietly. "A certain portion of the money you give to church every Sunday is put into a disaster relief fund. When a disaster like this happens, within hours our relief organization flies in blankets, clothing, tents, and food. When we all work together through the church, we can do a lot."

"Wow!" Tim said. His eyes were shining. "That makes me feel like going out and getting some more customers for my newspaper route so I'll have more to give!"

 We are thankful that you have blessed us so much, dear Lord, that it is possible for us to give to those in need. Help us to be generous.

Can you find an article in a newspaper or a church magazine telling about someone helping others in need?

■ HOW MUCH MONEY?

Matt. 6:24-34: "be concerned above everything else with the Kingdom of God and with what he requires of you, and he will provide you with all these other things" (v. 33).

How much money do we really need?" Dad asked at dinner.

"Why?" Lois wanted to know.

"I have an offer of a job promotion," Dad said. "I would earn four thousand more a year. But I would either have to travel and be away from home for weeks, or else we would have to move."

"I want you home," Lois said. "I can get a job cutting our neighbor's lawn. And I can do more baby-sitting."

"Where would we move?" Tim asked.

Dad named the city. "The nearest seminary is 75 miles away. It would be difficult for Mom to continue working for her degree. I would hate to see her give up her dream."

"I'm saving my paper money to buy my own car," Tim said. "And soon I'll be old enough to get a better-paying job."

The Simons talked some more. They all felt it was more important to have Dad spend time with the family than for them to buy a microwave oven or more expensive cars or put in a swimming pool. All of them were happy when Dad decided to decline the promotion.

 So many times, Lord Jesus, we have to decide what is most important. Give us wisdom at these times.

Discuss what decision you would have made if you had been the Simons. Talk about what the most important things are for your family.

■ SNIFF! SNIFF!

1 Cor. 3:16-23: "Surely you know that you are God's temple and that God's Spirit lives in you!" (v. 16).

Mom sniffed as Tim walked in the family room. She got up, walked over to Tim, put her face down close to his jacket, and sniffed again. Then she stepped back, put her hands on her hips and said, "Timothy Andrew Simon!"

Tim played dumb. "What's wrong, Mom?"

Dad reached over and switched off the TV.

"I smoked at one time," he said calmly. Noticing Tim's startled expression, he continued, "You don't remember. I stopped when you were little. Mom never did like my cigarettes and pipe smelling up the car and house. Then doctors started to talk about smoking and cancer, and one of my friends got throat cancer. I began to ask myself if I was taking good care of the body God had given me." Dad paused. "But in the end it was just a silly little thing that made me stop. Mom and I didn't have much money those days. I had just bought a new suit and was wearing it. I was carrying you and trying to smoke. You were wriggling, and somehow ashes dropped into my suit and burned a hole right in front. I got it mended, but it always showed a little." Dad smiled. "I guess I have you to thank, Tim, that I got rid of both a costly and a dirty habit."

Dear God, thank you for our wonderful bodies. Help us to take good care of them in every way.

Look at some cigarette ads together. Do they tell the whole truth? What devices are used to get people to think it's smart to smoke?

■ SHARED EXPERIENCES

Luke 2:41-52:   "Every year the parents of Jesus went to Jerusalem for the Passover Festival. When Jesus was twelve years old, they went to the festival as usual" (vv. 41-42).

The yearly trip to Jerusalem must have been an exciting event for Jesus," Dad said. "The journey on foot took two or three days, but Jesus and his parents would be traveling with neighbors and friends, so that would be a fun experience. Then what a thrill to catch sight of the holy city and the dome of the temple glittering in the sun! Pilgrims from everywhere jostled each other in the streets. The ceremonies at the temple must have impressed both observers and participants: the trumpets calling the worshipers, the sweet smell of incense, the bleating of sheep to be offered as sacrifices, the white-robed priests chanting, the blood flowing. On the journey home and for many days after that, Jesus and his parents must have discussed what they had seen.

"Going to Jerusalem together was just one religious experience Jesus and his parents shared," Dad continued. "These shared experiences glued the family together. Our family has shared religious experiences too."

"Our prayer time," Lois said.

"Christmas!" Tim spoke up.

"Holy Week services," Lois remembered.

"Special prayers for us when we have a birthday," Tim said. Then he grinned and added, "And Sunday dinners—they're always good."

Dear God, thank you for shared experiences as a family.

Talk about your family's shared experiences. Are there more things you could be doing together?

■ DISCOURAGED KIDS

Col. 3:18-21: "Parents, do not irritate your children" (v. 21).

The phone rang. Tim picked it up.

"Huh? Oh, yeah. Yeah, I'll tell Mom. OK. Bye."

He replaced the phone on its hook and sat slumped in his chair.

"Dad," he said. "He won't be home for dinner again tonight. Working, he said. Guess . . . ," he cleared his throat, "guess he forgot my ball game."

Lois walked into the room, and Tim punched her in the stomach. She doubled up, then came back at him. Grabbing a fistful of his red hair, she shook his head.

"Ouch! That hurts," Tim shrieked.

"You little beasts!" Mom yelled, and then she put her hand over her mouth, amazed at what she had said.

"Well, so what?" Lois said, backing off. "Dad and you never have time for us any more. Dad and his work. You and your church. We hardly ever eat together any more."

"Yeah, and Dad doesn't even care about my ball games," Tim complained.

Later that evening when Dad arrived the Simon family had a long talk together. Everyone agreed that they were not spending enough time together.

"We'll all make time for our family because it's our family that loves us the most, and it's there we can learn how to become the people God wants us to be," Dad said, and everybody smiled.

Dear God, help us to value our family and give time to each other.

Set aside one night a week for family time. Take turns planning what to do that night.

■ MEN DON'T CRY

John 11:17-37:   "Jesus wept" (v. 35).

Dad's brother had died from a heart attack. Dad had come home from work and was packing his suitcase to fly to be with the family. His face was gray, and he looked like an old, old man.

"You'd feel better if you cried a little," Mom said.

"I can't," Dad said. "All the time I was growing up, people told me, 'Boys don't cry. Men don't cry.' I've held my tears back so long now I don't know how to let them go."

"But Jesus cried," Mom protested. "Jesus was a man, and he cried."

"I know, I know," Dad said. "I don't believe any more that men shouldn't cry. It's just that I don't seem able to. But one thing's for sure," he said, brushing back his hair from his eyes, "I'm going to let Tim cry when he feels like crying." Then a tear escaped and trickled down his cheek, and when Mom reached over to kiss it away, he began to sob.

Dear God, we thank you for the gift of tears, which helps pressure to escape and makes us feel better when we are hurting.

Do you know someone who is feeling bad about something? Send them a card telling them that you care.

■ WHAT HAPPENS WHEN WE DIE?

1 Cor. 15:42-58: "Death gets its power to hurt from sin, and sin gets its power from the Law. But thanks be to God who gives us the victory through our Lord Jesus Christ!" (vv. 56-57)

That night after Dad had left to be with his brother's family, the children and Mom were sitting at the dinner table.

"What happens when people die?" Tim asked.

"Physically," Mom said, "the body ceases to function. The heart doesn't pump blood through the body anymore. Without oxygen from the blood the brain quits working. It's like turning off the key to a car engine. Everything stops.

"But we're more than our bodies," Mom continued. "We have spirits too that live in our bodies. When we die, our spirits leave our bodies."

"Wow!" Lois said. "Where do they go?"

"The Bible isn't specific about that," Mom said, "except to tell us God takes care of our spirits."

"Guess that should be enough," Lois said, "but it's sure mysterious, isn't it?"

Dear God, we thank you that we can trust you to take care of us both in life and death.

Go for a walk in a cemetery. Notice the names and dates on the tombstones. How old were the people when they died? Why do you think they died?

■ EATING RIGHT

1 Kings 19:1-8: "Get up and eat, or the trip will be too much for you" (v. 7).

Tim couldn't wake up in the mornings, so his dad bought him a clock radio. Tim slept through the music. His mother called him. Tim fell right back to sleep. Every morning he came tearing downstairs with two minutes left to get to school. When Tim's progress card came, his dad wanted to talk with him.

"You haven't been doing well in math," Dad observed. "I see math is right before lunch."

"So?" Tim asked.

"You don't put gas in your tank in the morning," Dad said. "Your engine sputters and misses through the first hours, and then finally dies altogether."

"What do you mean?"

"You don't eat breakfast. Tim, if we don't eat properly, we can't do good work. Son, we just have to take good care of our bodies, getting enough sleep and proper food. I have a feeling that you've been staying up too late at night. So there'll be no TV in your room until you've had a month of getting up on time and eating your breakfast."

Dear God, help us to take good care of our bodies and minds so they will remain healthy.

Talk about health habits that your family needs to establish.

■ WHEN YOU'RE SCARED

Psalm 27: "The Lord is my light and my salvation; I will fear no one" (v. 1).

The newspapers had carried accounts of arrests made in a junior high school of people who were selling drugs to students.

"I see this one guy almost every day when Brian and I go to the park for softball practice," Tim said. "He says he lights up after school. Says it gives him a real good feelin'. He just doesn't worry about anything then."

"What does he have to worry about?" Mom asked.

"I asked him one day. He said his parents have divorced, that he never sees his dad, and his mom yells at him all the time. He said what's the use of going to school when the whole world is going to be blown up anyway? He just wants to forget it all."

"What a sad way to handle problems," Dad said. "How much better to take our problems to God and ask him to work things out. No matter how discouraging things look, God can always help us. To turn to drugs is foolish. Soon that boy will not be able to live without drugs, and his whole life will be ruined. Tim, I know a group that works with boys like him. Next time you see him in the park, why don't you ask him if he wants help?"

Dear God, help us to have eyes to see those who are worried and discouraged so we can tell them about you.

Does your family know the facts about drugs? Do you know where to refer people who need help getting off drugs?

105

■ PLAY FAIR

Amos 5:21-24: "let justice flow like a stream, and righteousness like a river that never goes dry" (v. 24).

Mom, could Ann stay overnight with me sometime?" Lois asked. "She was crying again in school today."'

Mom looked up.

"She had on a pair of pants that looked kinda funny," Lois went on, "and the kids teased her. She told me afterward she hates her clothes. Her Mom gets most of them at thrift stores."

"Is her father out of work?" Mom asked.

"He ran away two years ago. Her mom works. But there are five kids in the family. Her mother has a real good job. But she gets paid only half what the man who had her job before got, because she's a woman. Why is that, Mom?"

"I guess years ago people thought that since men had to support their families, they should be paid enough to do that. Married women's work was thought of as extra income."

"But it doesn't seem fair, Mom, if Ann's mother does the same work the man did but she gets paid less."

"It isn't fair, Lois. Let's have both Ann and her mother over and see what we can do. If what she says is true, her employer is probably breaking the law."

Dear God, help us always to be fair and just in our business dealings.

Do you have a woman secretary working in your church? Does she get paid a fair wage with benefits?

■ THIS LITTLE LIGHT OF MINE

Isa. 9:2-7: "The people who walked in darkness have seen a great light" (v. 2).

The Simons were driving home from a midnight Christmas service at church.

"Mom, why do all of us light little candles and hold them?" Lois wanted to know.

"Lighting candles is picture language," Mom explained. "The world is a dark place. People live in darkness. Jesus said that as long as he was in the world, he was the light of the world. He said after he left, we were to be lights."

"How can we be lights?" Lois asked.

"Both by what we don't do and what we do," Mom said. "If we don't lie or steal or cheat, we are lights. And if we are kind and just and helpful and honest and love, we are lights."

"I hope I always am a light," Lois said.

We thank you, Jesus, that you were willing to come to earth to show us the way.

Put a candle on the table to remind you of Jesus the Light of the world. Talk about ways you were a light today.

■ FROM THE BOTTOM OF MY HEART

Psalm 103: "Praise the Lord, my soul! All my being, praise his holy name!" (v. 1).

The Simon's TV hadn't been working for a whole month. Tim and Lois had found other things to do. They discovered interesting books at the library. Tim got his electric train running. Lois learned to sew. Both of them put the pictures from their summer's vacation in albums. But they still missed having a TV.

Christmas morning there was a big white package under the tree marked, "For the Simon Family." Tim ripped off the paper wrappings. Dad helped him get out the big staples holding down the cover. Tim peered in. Then he raised his arms and said, "A TV! Praise the Lord!"

Mom and Dad didn't laugh. They knew Tim was thanking God from the bottom of his heart, and they were happy it was the first thing he thought to do.

Dear God, forgive us when we forget to thank you for all the good things you give us.

Go around the table several times saying, "Thank you, God, for _____."

108

■ SPACE TO GROW

Isa. 40:28-31: "those who trust in the Lord for help will find their strength renewed" (v. 31).

Mom opened her Christmas present from Dad and found a pair of mittens.

"How nice!" she said and slipped one on. "Oh, what's this?"

She took out a piece of paper and unfolded it. It was an airline ticket for her to fly back the next day and spend Christmas with her father and mother! Mom started to laugh and cry.

"But what will *you* do?" she asked Dad.

Dad smiled. "We've taken care of everything. Don't worry about us. Just enjoy your time with your mom and dad."

All of us need time away from our family, time when we can be free and just do what we want to do. Even Jesus took his disciples away on little "vacations" from time to time, to the mountains or to the lake.

Jesus said, "Let us go off by ourselves to some place where we will be alone and you can rest a while" (Mark 6:31).

Sometimes, however, spending time with others can draw us closer to God. Whether we are alone or with others, the important thing is to take time to be refreshed and become stronger Christians.

Dear God, thank you for times when we can be by ourselves without having to think about work.

Does each member of your family have some free time every week? Can you plan your schedule so this will be possible?

■ FAMILY TIME AT HOME

Deut. 4:1-14: "Tell your children and your grandchildren" (v. 9).

Marian's so lucky," Lois said unexpectedly one night as they were eating dinner.

"Why?" Mom asked. "How is she lucky?"

"Her folks stay home every Monday night and play games with their kids," Lois explained. "She says they have a good dinner together first. Then they build a fire in the fireplace and play games or sing or read or pop corn. She says they always end by reading the Bible together. They've finished reading many books in the Bible. Marian says it's the best time all week long."

Mom and Dad looked at each other.

The next evening Dad asked, "What if we set aside Sunday as family day? We can take turns planning what to do together."

Tim looked dismayed, but then his face brightened. "When it's my turn to choose, can we all go to a ball game together?"

Dad grinned. "Sure, why not? If you'll go to a concert with me once in a while."

"I want to go to church at least some Sunday evenings," Mom said.

"I want to stay home and read or sing or play games together," Lois objected.

"We'll take turns planning our Sundays," Dad said once again. "But we should always include some activities that will draw us closer, both to each other and to the Lord Jesus."

 Dear heavenly Father, thank you for families.

Consider setting aside your own family day.

BIBLE READINGS SERIES

Bible Readings for Women
    Lyn Klug
Bible Readings for Men
    Steve Swanson
Bible Readings for Parents
    Ron and Lyn Klug
Bible Readings for Couples
    Margaret and Erling Wold
Bible Readings for Singles
    Ruth Stenerson
Bible Readings for Families
    Mildred and Luverne Tengbom
Bible Readings for Teenagers
    Charles S. Mueller
Bible Readings for Mothers
    Mildred Tengbom
Bible Readings for Teachers
    Ruth Stenerson
Bible Readings for Students
    Ruth Stenerson
Bible Readings for the Retired
    Leslie F. Brandt
Bible Readings for Church Workers
    Harry N. Huxhold
Bible Readings for Office Workers
    Lou Ann Good
Bible Readings for Growing Christians
    Kevin E. Ruffcorn
Bible Readings for Caregivers
    Betty Groth Syverson
Bible Readings for Troubled Times
    Leslie F. Brandt
Bible Readings for Farm Living
    Frederick Baltz
Bible Readings on Prayer
    Ron Klug
Bible Readings on Hope
    Roger C. Palms
Bible Readings on God's Creation
    Denise J. Williamson